I0642758

COMSTOCK
PHANTOMS

COMSTOCK PHANTOMS

Copyright ©2004 by Brian David Bruns

All photography, interior, and cover design by Brian David Bruns

All rights reserved. Printed and bound in the United States of America. No part of this publication may be reproduced or transmitted in any form or by any means, electronic or mechanical, including photocopy, recording, or any information storage and retrieval system— except by a reviewer who may quote brief passages in a review to be printed in a magazine, newspaper, or the Web— without permission in writing from the publisher. For information, contact via lovebruns@yahoo.com, or write P.O. Box 277, Hiawatha, IA 52233-0277.

Although the author and publisher have made every effort to ensure the accuracy and completeness of information contained in this book, we assume no responsibility for errors, inaccuracies, omissions, or any inconsistency herein. Any slights of people, places, or organizations are unintentional.

Businesses reflect the time of publishing. All references to businesses mentioned herein are merely the opinion of the author, and in no way represent the beliefs and/or practices of said business and/or owner.

First Printing 2003
Second Printing 2004

LCCN 2003097276

ISBN 0-9745217-1-X

ATTENTION SCHOOLS, UNIVERSITIES, COLLEGES, AND LIBRARIES: Quantities of this book are available for educational purposes. Special books or book excerpts can also be created to fit specific needs. For information, please contact publisher.

TABLE OF CONTENTS

ACKNOWLEDGEMENTS

*Many thanks to an unparalleled assembly of friends:
Alma, Daniel, Kimmy, Mihaela, Will, and of course Ken.*

INTRODUCTION

I have always found the supernatural to be intriguing. Over the years I have collected much literature on the various unexplained phenomena of our culture. I take pleasure in reading of such strange and bizarre encounters as ghosts, poltergeists, UFOs, mysterious creatures, spontaneous human combustion... etc. Equally interesting to me, however, is the debunking of such myth and material. I have satisfied myself with the disengaged, harmless pastime of armchair adventure regarding these occurrences... but no more.

When visiting the Old Washoe Club with a friend in 1999, we were both intrigued by the history of the old building. I strode confidently back to view the renowned spiral staircase. Turning to comment upon this to my friend, I noted she was absent. Looking about, I realized she had not crossed under the archway to view the stairs at all.

I asked her what was the matter, and she calmly replied she would not take another step forward. She felt something was very wrong here, and was fine waiting for me at the bar. I was quite surprised not only by her words, but by her matter-of-fact attitude. I asked her if she were somehow afraid, and she replied in her usual pragmatic way she was not. She just knew she was unwelcome, and she heeded that. We soon discovered that the place was considered quite haunted by many, many people.

This encounter, and even another that very day, affected me. In fact, it annoyed me. I had always been intrigued by these phenomena, yet was apparently not able to experience them when those around me could. It was then I decided to investigate further.

They say those who forget the past are doomed to repeat it. I have found Virginia City to be a rare place where the forgotten past is repeated... all by itself.

-Brian David Bruns

CAVEATS

ABOUT THE HAUNTS

I feel a word or two is called for in regards to the tales. These stories are meant to entertain the reader, perhaps even to frighten. I interviewed many people to gather these tales. Most of the stories were freely hurled at me, unsolicited, at the very mention of a collection of ghost stories. People enjoy sharing these stories as much as they enjoy hearing them.

Many of the stories, therefore, include the actual names of actual people and, at least in their minds, actual events. It is not my place to judge the merit of their words based on probability. I did, however, make judgments based on readability. While editing I took the liberty of slashing details I found irrelevant or unworkable. Indeed, I even combined different stories from different people into a single narrative, just to capture all the many ways in which spirits choose to manifest themselves. Some of the contributors to these tales will undoubtedly read them and lament, "This is not what I said." Others will hopefully comment, "This is better than what I said."

When enthralled by the dark words of a storyteller, lit menacingly by the flickering campfire on a chilly autumn night, no one cares if a few details were intentionally rearranged. These stories, through their editing, have become my stories. This is not without precedent. It was here, in Virginia City in the 1860's, after all, where Mark Twain developed his infamous writing style. Like Mark Twain, I see no reason why I should let the truth get in the way of a good story.

ABOUT THE HISTORIES

I took great pains to make my short histories as accurate as possible. These passages are designed to add flavor to the settings of these stories, and to educate the reader about the fascinating history of the Comstock. No feverish exhuming of forgotten lore was involved in the drafting of these histories. They are designed as readable, short accounts with as much data as possible. Only relevant information is focused upon, or particularly interesting facts and occurrences. They are by no means exhaustive in any way.

Much of the histories are word of mouth, or information passed down from generation to generation. These words come from those who love this city and all of its glorious past. One can only accept such words at face value. When data comes from the efforts of other professionals, it is acknowledged. There is a wealth of information available to those who wish to seek it. The list of works cited in this book provides an excellent guide to some of those gems so rich in history.

ABOUT THE HUNTS

I do not necessarily believe in ghosts, nor do I disbelieve. I possess a scientific and primarily rational attitude towards such things, though I want to believe. I am quite unaware of anything spiritual in this world, even when those around me can unanimously feel a presence. Indeed, the house in which I resided in Reno for several years possessed a spirit of some sort, according to my roommates. A dog, they claimed it was, or a small child. It was a happy spirit that could be occasionally sensed in the newer, sunny parts of the house... not the older brick end that oozes character. Our four cats didn't seem to mind this entity, perhaps further emphasizing benevolence. Did I sense anything over the years? Certainly not.

My poor abilities to sense things, or even be aware of what's going on around me have been the subject of much mockery and ridicule, in fact. So who am I to undertake the responsibility of observing a ghost? My logic is pretty simple and painfully sound: if I can see it, then anyone can.

Most of the time people comment that if you look hard enough for something, you will find it, or at least think you did. In regards to this undertaking, I pose the opposite theory: if you try so hard to find something so fleeting and shy, it will not happen. As I plunge into these hunts with all the subtlety and grace of a Neandertal, I am quite sure if anything is generating fear in others... it is I. I am not a slick ghost-hunting expert, nor am I a University-sponsored parapsychologist. I am more a blundering fool, or amateur barbarian. My hapless adventures are undertaken with the right spirit (no pun intended), however, and should be enjoyed as such.

I should also mention many of these quests were executed with the support (and patience!) of property owners and local law enforcement. Nearly all of the places to which I refer are privately owned, and should be respected as such. It is my wish that everyone feel free to investigate the various businesses I have discussed, or to seek those who can further educate about the area. I do not recommend or endorse anyone's ambitions to crawl beneath buildings in search of forgotten burials, or scale down into abandoned mine shafts. Such activities are foolish and dangerous.

I

THE PIONEER EMPORIUM

"Battle Born", the motto of Nevada, was due to its start during the Civil War. In fact, Nevada has suffered less war casualties than almost any other state.

The façade of the Pioneer Emporium has been handsomely refinished in complimentary shades of green. Folded neatly beside the fifteen-foot high front windows are huge iron shutters... remnants from another era of security needs. The second story has also been refinished in greens, with a small table and chairs sitting idly on a deck overlooking C Street. Inside is a comfortable store with high wooden ceilings, lined with warm browns and wooden appointments. The smell of leather goods permeates the air, and Native American crafts, knives, and else further fill the Emporium.

THE HAUNTINGS

I was counting my register, closing up the shop with Patty. It was only about 5:30 PM, but since it was late October the sun was already setting. Being on the eastern slope of Mt. Davidson anyway, the sun had long ago stopped shining on the old buildings of Virginia City. The front door was finally closed, after having been open to invite customers in all day. This left the store very quiet. The tourists were no longer plodding along on the age-old, loose planks of the boardwalk. Those sounds had been resounding in our ears all day. In fact, even the nightly winds had not kicked in that night, so the only sounds were of Patty and me counting cash and clinking coin. We were both behind separate counters, which lined the main route through the store. I noted her frowning down at her register in concentration opposite me.

A different clicking sound caught my ear, and I casually looked up. The sound came from my left, in the main open area in the back of the store, near the big belt rack. This rack was a huge metal beast nearly four feet tall and a full five feet wide. It was loaded with literally a hundred or more belts. This thing was of thick, solid metal… it *had* to be to support such a load of leather belts. The clanking specifically emanated from it.

I was shocked to see all the belts swooshing from side to side. Obviously there was no way those belts could have started moving like that on their own, but there was no wind in the store at all. Even had the door been open and the usual strong winds been blowing in, they *still* would not have moved like that so far back in the store. There were a *hundred* belts swinging in unison! They slid

back and forth along the metal support pole in their swaying, clicking buckle against buckle. A cacophony of dull clacking sounded below as the loose ends of the belts slapped each other in their dance. That odd sound was very out of place in the silent store... and most unwelcome.

As if this were not odd enough, I saw the area near the belt rack growing blurry. Inexplicable wavy lines shimmered and shifted in front of the belt rack, just like heat waves over searing hot concrete. This occurrence was focused, however, and not broad like the summer horizon. They shifted together as a whole... and slowly detached themselves from the rack.

I hurriedly glanced around the entire store. Was I growing faint? Perhaps my blurring vision and imagination were rioting together for some unknown reason. The wavering emanation was localized though, and even more convincing was Patty. She was staring, mouth awkwardly open, at the *exact* same spot I was. The strange vision floated away from the big belt rack and moved through the store at a moderate speed. As it eased towards the front door, it passed between the two counters where Patty and I stood ogling. Our eyes met, widened in recognition of each other's awareness, then riveted back to the slowly moving mystery. As it passed by me and neared the front door, the waviness faded until there was nothing there at all. I stared in stunned silence at the spot I last saw the anomaly.

Silence reigned for several moments. Finally Patty asked in a halting voice, "Did you see what I saw?" She was obviously as shaken as I was. Her face was pale. I noticed some mangled dollar bills still in her clenched hand.

"I don't know," I responded honestly. I cautiously

whispered back, "What did you see?"

"You didn't see the man walk by?"

I stared at her incredulously, and a chill wracked my body. "The... *man?*"

She nodded. "He was standing next to the belt rack, and then walked through it, as if it weren't there. He was tall and thin. I didn't really make out his features, but he wore a white shirt with black pants. His clothes were period... and I think he had on black boots. He walked right in front of us towards the door!"

Despite my curiosity, I don't know if I would have been happier seeing the full man or not!

***

"Several times, inside the store, during the winter when the doors were shut, normally, we would smell pipe smoke... a wonderful smell. And a couple times we went outside and said, 'OK, who's got a pipe?' ...and there was no one there. You could kind of feel the presence. I don't know what the history of him and the store was, but I remember one day that stuff was just broken. I was totally upset. 'OK, fine. We can share this space, but you can't break my stuff. And if you're gonna break my stuff, then you have to go.' Nothing else was broken [after that], but we would very, very often smell pipe smoke.

And a girl who worked with me up there saw him. He had a black hat on, and a black coat. A gentleman. And kind... [he] wasn't mean. Not mean, just kind of mischievous. I never encountered him, but I smelled the pipe a lot."

The Hauntings

***

I was working late one night, and had just finished up. After several long hours of staring into numbers written on ledgers, I rubbed my eyes. I enjoyed the pleasant burning sensation of them being closed after so long, and just listened. The whistling of the winds through the streets sounded faintly outside. After a moment or two, I turned my head to look out the windows to C Street. It was dark outside, but the light of the gas lamps burned a warm, soft yellow. A few drunken revelers strolled by, and I listened as their laughter grew and then faded.

I quickly tidied up the top of the desk. I pulled the corner of a fat ledger from beneath the delicate foot of a tall doll that stood on the countertop next to the register. It seemed appropriate that this very expensive, well-dressed doll would hold down the corner of the sales ledger with a selfish, child-like stamp of her foot. After removing the ledger, I carefully ensured its balance was not compromised. It was a very expensive doll, over two feet tall and wearing a frilly Victorian dress, white stockings, and handcrafted boots of white silk. A white ribbon held back her thick blond curls. It cost several hundred dollars, so the last thing I wanted was to have it fall over. The doll was very stable, however, and of exquisite craftsmanship. That was why it stood on the counter, in fact, to ensure its safety.

I grabbed my coat and keys, then snapped off the lights. Fatigued, I trudged to the door and stepped out into the crisp night air. I made a last glance through the dark interior as I latched the door shut. I frowned. Something felt wrong. The pale yellow gaslight only illuminated the corner of the store, so the shadows were oppressive and deep. I couldn't see anything in there, and the unknown hung oppressively over the blackness like a gargoyle.

Shrugging it off, I turned to leave and reached to slip the keys into my purse. It wasn't there.

That's what was wrong! I forgot my purse.

I turned about and fumbled the keys back into the lock. I swung the door open, stepped into the dark shop... then stopped abruptly. Something *else* felt very wrong... and it wasn't my having forgotten my purse behind the counter.

My eyes locked onto something unusual in the edge of the soft light. Something large and white caught my eye. The hair on the back of my neck started to prickle. It was the doll. She was on the floor, by the counter. She hadn't fallen, however.

The doll was standing on the floor, fully erect... facing the door... and me. She was on the opposite side of the register than when I locked the door not fifteen seconds before. Adrenaline burst through me, and I whirled around and slammed the door shut, frantically locking it behind me. After I heard the latch click shut, I stared through the window into the darkness, my heart painfully pounding.

In the edge of the light, I could see her figure standing there, staring at the door. Locked door or not, I still ran most of the way home.

***

The Hauntings

"I remember that there was a ghost in there that would whisper my name. I could never tell if it was a male or female voice... but it was cold and clear. It would say my name, right next to my ear. Even if I were in a corner, I would hear it right behind me and right next to my ear. It was creepy."

***

I was finishing up work one day, doing the paperwork. It had been a busy day, and I was working pretty late. It was dark out, anyway, and most of the tourists were gone... or in the bars, I guess. It had been an unusually hot day, and the shop had been uncomfortable for a long, long time. After moving so much inventory and dealing with so many people, I felt beaten down. I was no longer hot, as the nights up in the mountains are always cool, but I felt grungy and unclean after hours of sweating had dried on me.

Anyway, as I was working I heard this sort of grinding sound... like something heavy sliding on stone. I looked around the shop. It was bright but silent, almost brooding. I felt very alone, suddenly. There was an incredible variety of miscellany before me, and I had to peer past upright stands and squint over racks of coats. I didn't see anything moving, though. I went back to work.

Several minutes passed as I worked wearily on the papers before me. I ran my fingers through my matted hair to get it out of my eyes. My forehead felt tacky from congealed sweat. What is worse than doing mentally taxing paperwork when you are tired and feeling nasty?

The strange grinding sound caught my ear again. It only lasted for perhaps a second, maybe two.

I looked up again. Nothing appeared amiss. I started to move from behind the counter and take a look around, but I stopped in mid-step. I was nearly finished, and just wanted to go home and take a shower! I shrugged off the inexplicable noise, and returned to the papers. As I stepped back before my work once again, I heard the sound once more.

Suddenly I was hit from behind... hard. I was pummeled on my left arm, my shoulders, and the base of my neck. I heard the sound of crashing pottery. I screamed, mostly from surprise, and I spun around... but there was nothing there. A cloud of dust billowed up around me and clung to my sweaty face. I blinked hard and repeatedly to get the grit from my eyes. The dull pummeling was immediately replaced with smarting pangs of pain. I stepped back, and my foot nearly slipped on something.

On the floor behind me were the remains of three ceramic pots. I immediately recognized they had fallen off the shelf above me. The thick, ragged edges of the shards were sharp and revealed just how heavy those pots had been before their fall.

Now, there are lots of pots for sale on the shelves, but they are all pushed way back from the edge so they don't break. I mean, there are earthquakes every now and then, and things can fall down if they are not specifically placed away from the edge.

I know *something* pushed those three, heavy pots off the shelf to try and hit me. I always felt that something in the store didn't like me, and this proved it. This has never happened to anybody *else*. Those pots were way too big

and heavy to move on their own. I wasn't hurt, though. Just shaken up… and angry.

***

I came in to work one day, and went to the back room. This room is packed with boxes, some open and some not, and hundreds of various piles of merchandise. The many shelves are lined with things, including a number of dolls in boxes or wrapped loosely in plastic. Their hard, glass eyes stared dully at me, warped through the layers of bubble wrap.

There on the floor were a couple of the dolls. They are expensive dolls, and are stored in the back so nobody messes with them or damages them. They're usually stored pretty well so they don't fall over or anything. I was more than annoyed to see two of them face down on the floor with their little arms stretched out towards the door of the shop. I noticed one of them, the doll with the tight brunette curls, had lost her little red shoe. I frowned down on them, almost like a mother standing over misbehaving children.

I'd just arrived, and decided to fix them after I had gone to the bathroom. I strode into the attached bathroom and closed the door behind me. With my mind a million miles away, I sat down on the toilet and thought about the busy day I had before me.

Then I heard the whisper.

I immediately became alert. I was the only one in the store. I had the only key to get in, in fact. The owners were out of town. It was not a voice from outside I heard… it was a faint whispering, like children conspiring behind the backs of adults. I leaned forward, straining to hear more, but could not. After another moment or two, I leaned back and stared blandly at the small bathroom I was in. I began to feel very awkward in here, and vulnerable.

Suddenly the bathroom door flung itself open and slammed against the wall so hard the mirror shook and a picture actually fell off the wall. I screamed in shock as the shards of glass rained over my ankles and filled my jeans with splinters and dust. My heart was instantly pounding painfully in my chest, and I absently flung my arms out to grasp the sink next to me, as if I needed stabilization!

My ragged breath sawed through the silence, but I swear I heard the faint sound of giggles. Time ticked by, and nothing else happened. I sat there, half naked and on the toilet, with the door wide open… but was too scared to move. After some time, the throbbing in my chest slowed, and I was left to analyze the splinters and rubble in my jeans.

I spent a few minutes kicking my jeans about, and eventually had to remove my shoes and actually shake out my pants to get all the small splinters out. The broken picture frame sat crookedly on the floor, feeling guilty. My fright was quickly being replaced by anger, as I had to deal with the situation.

When I finally exited the bathroom, I tentatively took a peek out. The first thing I noticed was that the dolls were no longer on the floor. Both of them were *standing up*, on the shelf where they were supposed to be… but facing the bathroom door. I felt like they were waiting for me to come out, to silently mock the butt of their cruel joke. I began to shiver in a slow, building fright.

On the floor, in the middle of the room and far, far away from the shelves, was still a small red shoe.

***

The sun was streaming into the store, and it was a warm, glorious morning in July. The weather had been perfect lately, not too hot and not too cool. Up this high in the mountains, the weather tends to be mellower than in the surrounding deserts. It was early morning, and I was wandering through the store setting things aright and doing the usual prep for what promised to be a very busy day.

One shelf in the front of the store, behind one of the counters, was rearranged oddly, I noticed. The sun was hitting the shelf full on, and all the little objects, mostly knick-knacks and little ceramics, were all turned about to face the wall. That was weird, as no one had rearranged yesterday to my knowledge. Honestly, there are so many stories of spirits mischievously moving things about I just sighed and manually turned them all around.

The sun was getting very warm on my left side as I finished rotating them all, and I felt a thump on my shoulder. I turned to see who was there, but was greeted only with blaring sun in my eyes. I squeezed my eyes shut, and snapped a hand up to block the rays. When I opened them again, brilliant reds swam across my vision and blurred everything. However, I saw something unmistakably peculiar.

There, in the window leading to C Street, was a vision of some sort. I can think of no other way to describe it. Floating among all the red swirlies left by the sun was a clear scene of letters, big and bold, that spelled a message. I couldn't make it out. Nearby was a key of some sort. I had the strong impression this was an outdoor scene, and the key would lead to something that had been locked for many years. Inside this thing was a small, hideous face that made me shudder, though it wasn't grimacing or anything.

That was it. The vision disappeared and I was left with a blinding vision of C Street. I knew I was meant to see this... vision... and something was trying to tell me something. That's why it moved the stuff on the shelf, and actually nudged me.

I was spooked from it, but customers started coming in really early that day, and I had little time to think about it. In the early afternoon, I managed to get a break with another employee, Rhonda.

"Rhonda," I started slowly, after taking a long drag on my cigarette. "I saw something really weird this morning."

"What's that?" she asked absently. She was a very pragmatic woman of middle years and long, curly hair that had been dyed somewhere between red and black. She was fiddling with one of her large hoop earrings. I figured she was no-nonsense and could provide some rational course of action, assuming any were warranted.

"Well, when I came in, the shelf with the little jars above the register had everything facing the wrong way. When I was fixing it, I felt a push on my shoulder, and turned to see what it was. Then I saw a vision."

"A vision?"

"Yeah." I took another pull from my cigarette. "It was letters of some sort, big and simple, with a key next to them. I think they were outside, and the key seemed to be made for something that hasn't been opened for years."

"No kidding?" she asked, sipping from a Coke.

"Yeah, and there was this nasty little face inside whatever the key opened up. It was small and, I don't know, just ugly. It's about three inches in diameter, I think."

"Whoa, that's creepy, man."

"Tell me about it."

"What do you think it means?"

"I don't know. I got the impression that it had to do with this building, though. I don't think I've ever seen any letters outside, though."

"Well," Rhonda said thoughtfully, "in the front there are the letters of the foundry that made the façade of the building way back when."

I brightened. "Yeah, that's right! Let's go look."

"Sure."

I put out my cigarette and we reentered the store. We walked through the shop and out the front. The façade of the Emporium had recently been repainted in a series of greens and yellows. The pillars built into the façade had the stamp of the original foundry that built them. The letters were near the boardwalk, painted over but molded clearly into the pedestal.

PACIFIC COOPERATIVE FOUNDRY. Obviously this was not what we were looking for.

"Huh," she grunted, stumped. "Well, you should tell Jerry. He lives upstairs here, and he might know what you're talking about."

"Yeah," I agreed. "He might know what this locked thing is, too. He owns the whole building, after all."

"Right," she approved.

"Really?" Jerry asked, intrigued. We were both behind the counter, and I told him the whole story I had mentioned to Rhonda earlier. Jerry was about 50 years old, and had the gray hair to prove it, but was still very fit and energetic. He was also usually very excitable about these things. This was no exception. His moustache quivered with anticipation. He believes in ghosts, and had seen many in his days.

"Yeah, and I think the whole thing has to do with this building."

He frowned a moment. "You weren't here when we found the cabinet, were you?"

"What cabinet?"

"The old medicine cabinet that Pete and I found upstairs. It was a few years ago, but it was a really old cabinet, about three feet tall and maybe eighteen inches wide. It was only a few inches deep, so I thought it might be a medicine cabinet, though we don't know what it really is. It is pretty old, though we don't know how old, either. Pete is good at figuring these things out, and thinks it is at least eighty years old. We found it upstairs. It's locked still. We could never find the key."

I perked up. "That must be it! Can I see it?"

Jerry shrugged. "Sure. It's in the back room now."

Together we went into the back storage room, and Jerry started digging past various half-empty boxes filled with all manner of trinkets and merchandise. I could see what he was after, for in the corner was an antique-looking wooden cabinet. It looked like any other piece of old junk, and I had not noticed it before. It was way in the back, behind a bunch of things. After a few further moments he cleared the section before it and pulled it away from the wall. He was very careful in bringing it out into the room… he has a fondness for antiques and knows how to handle them.

He set it on a worktable, and wiped the dust off the top. It was simply carved, and had a very thick layer of old varnish on it. The varnish was now uneven and looked like honey smeared over the old wood, which was of poor quality. I could see why he didn't pursue the item any further. The base was all scratched up, too. The lock was built into the door, and was very small but sturdy in appearance.

"Is this it?" he asked.

"I didn't see what it was," I replied. "Just the key."

"Oh."

"That's really cool, though. And you don't know where the key is?"

He shook his head. "Never found it. I haven't looked for years."

"Well, now you know where to look. Know of any letters outside the building? Other than the foundry markings in the front."

Jerry frowned. "No, but I just might take a look."

"You should."

"Hey!"

I looked up to see Jerry striding in with excitement, beaming from ear to ear.

"Jerry, your mustache is quivering again. You know I get nervous when that happens."

He gave me a quick sour look. "I found some letters outside. Come on, take a look!"

Rhonda overheard this from the other counter, and

looked up from her work. "What kind of letters? Did you really?"

"Yeah! Watch things, while we take a look."

"Sure."

Both of us fairly ran towards the back of the building, up closer to B Street. It was still mid-afternoon, and the sun was high in the sky. The back of the building was in shadow, down below the street as it was. Jerry squatted down near a corner. He brushed aside some rough weeds, and pointed. There was an awkward transition from the building to some pavement that served no apparent purpose... the kind you expect from such an old building. A concrete section was angled down from the building. The flat patio crept up and over the bottom of this angled piece. Just where the patio overlapped the angled piece, the tops of a series of letters peeked over the lip. They were obviously fingered into the wet concrete when it was originally set many years ago.

"Wow! What now?"

Jerry looked up at me with surprise. "We pull up the edge of the concrete, obviously."

I chuckled.

"Seriously," he continued. "I'll get some tools from the main office. We can pry up this edge as far as the crack there. It shouldn't be that tough."

I shrugged in agreement. I wasn't feeling quite that ambitious, but I knew Jerry.

"Let's do it." I knew it was assured, once Jerry got excited. A few minutes later he was prying at the edge with a heavy pickaxe. He put his weight into it, and soon the concrete grudgingly gave a creak. A few minutes later, he managed to wriggle it back and forth to get the piece away from the base of the building. The section refused to actually be pulled up, for some reason. However, the letters were finally fully revealed.

MATT   STEPHANIE   6-13-02

"Huh," I grunted.

"Yeah," Jerry agreed. "I guess they either lived in the apartment or something when this was poured."

"Well, that wasn't very exciting."

Jerry smiled broadly. "No, but it *was* interesting."

I shrugged and started fishing for my pack of cigarettes. Jerry dropped and tried to wrestle the broken corner of the patio back into place. He suddenly gave a cry of excitement.

"Look at this!"

He gave the big, cracked stone a tug to the side. Barely visible, in the side of the concrete that had been scribed upon, was a small flash of metal. He fingered it a moment, and it became clearer.

A small key had been dropped into the wet concrete, just below the names of Matt and Stephanie.

He looked at me.

I looked at him.

"Damn."

Together we raced back into the Emporium. We both bolted past Rhonda, who looked up in surprise. She called out to us as we ran by, but we didn't respond, so intent were we on the cabinet in the back.

Jerry ran up to the cabinet and finally paused before it, holding the key nearby. Sure enough, it appeared to be a match. The metal, iron most likely, was the same as the lock itself, and the size was equal. With one last look at me, he stuck the key in and gave it a turn. It resisted at first, but with just a bit of force it turned with a very loud snap.

"Oh my God," murmured Rhonda from behind us. I turned and gave her a smile. I hadn't heard her follow us, and we all knew she should be watching the store, but no one said anything.

Jerry slowly and gently pulled open the medicine cabinet. The hinges were old and resisted, but a slow, even force overruled any objections. As soon as he opened it, the first thing I saw made my heart leap into my throat. Rhonda gave a gasp from behind me that almost made me jump.

In the top shelf of the cabinet was a doll's head. The big, painted eyes stared out at us past dirty, matted eyelashes sagging with ancient glue. There was no body, just the sagging, dirty head on a shelf… just like in the vision.

President Lincoln illegally allowed Nevada into statehood to ensure it was a pro-Union state (it did not constitutionally have enough residents for statehood).

THE HISTORY

This structure has always been a source of merchandise. One of the first elevators in the West was located here, allowing merchandise to be stored easily upstairs and brought down to the main C Street level upon need. Shipments were therefore received from B Street above in what have since become apartments.

When the current owners of the building took possession, it still retained the original electric wiring, complete with antique ceramic knobs and light fixtures. The original flooring lasted as late as the spring of 2001, when it had eroded too much for safety (as well as a need to replace the plumbing beneath). Like so many others, this building was rebuilt after the devastating fire of 1875.

A BREATH OF HELL (THE FIRE OF 1875)

"A breath of hell melted the main portion of the town to ruins. Accounts speak in amazement not only of the explosive combustion of the wood but also of the fact that even brick buildings seemed to wither into heaps of rubble at the diabolical onslaught.

"On all sides was heard the roar of the fire, the crash of falling roofs and walls, and every few minutes tremendous explosions of black and giant powder, as buildings were blown up in various parts of town...." [1]

During the heady days of the Comstock, Virginia City and Gold Hill endured dozens of fires. Money was flowing so freely that, even though entire residential areas and business blocks were annihilated, they were quickly rebuilt. Wooden side-by-side construction, coupled with the twenty-four hour operations of the mines requiring candle, oil lamp, or lantern light, as well as the arid climate, lack of water and the unstoppable Washoe Zephyr were just some of the reasons why fires were so common and so disastrous.

"From 1861 to 1866, seven volunteer fire companies were formed in Virginia City and three in Gold Hill. The competition between the fire companies was fierce, sometimes resulting in fights and riots to determine which company would occupy the best position to fight a particular fire." [2]

"In the midst of the troublous times, on October 26th, 1875, a mighty fire swept Virginia City. I remember that conflagration, for in it I lost everything I owned, including a trunkful of personal keepsakes, and my special pride, a pair of new gum-boots. But this fire brought about far more disastrous results, for it destroyed 2000 dwellings and many public buildings. It was my fate to be in the middle of flaming San Francisco in 1906 and the great Berkeley fire in 1923, in which 800 houses burned, but the intensity of that mining-camp blaze lingers in my memory as the fiercest of all. Mt. Davidson seemed bursting in volcanic eruption. [2]

"The fire had started in a small one-story lodging house on A Street kept by a woman named Kate Shay, well but not favorably known as Crazy Kate, and the flames spread with astounding rapidity. Only by heroic efforts were the mines saved, though many mills and hoisting-works went up in smoke." (3)

The fire was so great and displaced so many homes, the streets were filled with people hauling trunks full of mementos, bundles of clothing and bedding, and even furniture. They labored to save something, anything, from the unquenchable flames. More often than not, once they had set their burden in the frigid, muddy streets for a rest, the advancing flames would force them to abandon everything and beat a hasty retreat.

"The night of the fire, the zephyr returned in full force, knocking down remains of buildings, which were only standing walls with little supporting them. Before midnight, snow started to fall heavily. People remembered that Eilley Bowers, the Bonanza-queen-turned-pauper who had resorted to fortune-telling, had recently foretold that a fire would destroy the city and a big storm would follow." (4)

The fire cost the city more than $12 million. (5)

WORKS CITED

1. The Best of Virginia City and the Comstock, p.25
2. An Editor on the Comstock Lode, pp.120-121
3. Territorial Enterprise, Oct. 27, 1875
4. The Roar and the Silence, p.114
5. History of Nevada, 1881, p.598

II

THE GOLD HILL HOTEL

Eilley Bowers, a superstitious girl who believed she could read the future in a crystal ball, built a $300,000 mansion in Washoe Meadows with Comstock money. It boasted $3,000 worth of Venetian mirrors.

The hotel is elegant, the atmosphere is casual. The Great Room, patio and bar are perfect places to kick-back and enjoy. Connoisseurs of fine liquors will appreciate the hotel's selection of cognacs, single malt scotches, liqueurs, over forty-five beers and spirits of all types. Theatrical performances (from Cowboy experience to Shakespeare) are presented during the summer months. Special events such as book signings, chamber music or solo concerts occur throughout the year.

THE HAUNTINGS

I was working in the new section of the hotel, only recently built and perched neatly behind and above the original late 19th century structure. In the hallway near the door I encountered a very strong floral smell... roses, to be specific. It was quite powerful, but very pleasant. The occupant of the room, a middle-aged woman obviously from a larger city considering her dress, was leaving her room just as I happened by. I politely asked her, "What perfume are you wearing? It's very nice."

With some irritation she replied, "Nothing. I'm not wearing any."

She strode away curtly after that. I merely shrugged off the encounter, then entered her room to tidy it up. I stepped through the entrance and into the main chamber, which was large and quite nice. A huge fireplace dominated the left wall; stone from floor to ceiling and waiting patiently with logs ready to be lit. The ceilings were tall, and the glass door leading to the patio revealed little in the pre-dawn light beyond the scrub-studded hills in the distance. The ruined wreck of the Yellow Jacket mine reflected direct sunlight that had not yet touched the hotel itself as the sun just started to rise beyond the mountains.

The room was quiet and empty. I approached the bed to begin the usual duties of changing sheets, but something slowed my pace. The room felt... different. Naturally I was quite familiar with each of the rooms... I clean them all daily. But this room possessed something very different this time, something I had never before encountered. I felt...energy... permeating the space. It is very difficult to describe, but I felt some sort of static electricity, almost, and could sense it filling the entire room. Certainly it was all around the bed, where I needed to be. I stopped entirely and just gazed about, analyzing the experience.

I couldn't hear anything unusual in the silent room, but I could still smell the floral scent very strongly. My eyes scanned the chamber for any possible source: a vase, soaps, shampoos, lotions… anything. But I saw nothing of the sort. Besides, the smell was so dense and rich, it was not likely to be from anything so delicately scented. As I spent more time in the room, I felt this energy throb with discontent. It was not malevolent or angry… but it *was* displeased with my presence. I felt the vibes crawl across my skin, even though I had barely made it past the entranceway.

Firmly, I shrugged off the sensations and boldly strode towards the bed. These odd feelings were strong, but they were completely irrational, and I had work to do. I saw nothing, heard nothing. It was just my mind… and the smell, which could be absolutely anything.

I came within a few feet of the bed, and the pulsing energy seemed to gel in the air around me, then I felt the room thicken with annoyance. Each step was slower than the last, and I realized suddenly, without any doubt, I was *absolutely* not welcome here. My entire body shivered with the realization. Adrenaline sharply jerked through my spine, and I nearly jumped inadvertently as I whirled about and made for the door. I wasted no time in departing. My exit was swift and unobstructed. I left the door open, but did not look back. I still can't explain any of it.

***

I was closing up with Tina one night. It was a quiet night during winter, and there was no one in the bar or even the hotel. It was only mid-evening, but we were all closing up. It was the off-season anyway, so there were few people willing to brave the snow-gripped Sierra during the middle of that week. We were both chatting about nothing in particular, just passing the time as people do. We were in Room 4.

More specifically, we were both in the bathroom of Room 4. It was a dark chamber, though painted white as if to combat the effect of the ancient bricks, stone slab floor, and darkly polished wainscoting. There was a lot of character in the small room, though, and I found I enjoyed it. Tina was talking as she tidied up the sink in the corner. I was arranging the towels and the curtains around the tub, but stopped after a moment to gaze out the window.

The huge, ancient window revealed the north parking lot, the front porch and entrance to the hotel. The entire façade was lined with bright Christmas lights, which filled the entire area with an intense white glow off the rather deep snow. The wind whistled around the building, and blew diagonally across the porch. The snow, which had accumulated earlier in the day on top of the wooden rails, was soon sculpted into all sorts of interesting shapes by the wind. The wooden sign out front rocked back and forth from the incessant blowing, knocking its own Morse code against the bushes and posts.

Crossing my arms beneath my breasts, I leaned against the broken bricks of the walls. I enjoyed the warmth of the hotel, even though this was anything but efficient at keeping the winter chills at bay. Still, as cool as the room was, it was nothing compared to the night's freezing temperatures outside. The undulating snow banks slumped into the darkness beyond the reach of the cheering lights. I saw the others from the hotel trudging through the thick snow to their cars, bundled tightly against the oppressive cold. I would be winding my own way through the narrow and twisting roads before too long, and I handled the thought with dread. The drive was harrowing enough in the summer! But when snow shrouded the mountains, the huge drop-offs lining the crazily snaking roads seemed all too close for comfort.

"Viki."

I snapped my attention back to the present, and realized Tina's droning words had stopped. I waited a moment further for her to continue, but she did not. I glanced over to her. My gut lurched when I saw her there.

Her back was to the two mirrors in the corner. The effect was that I saw three different sides of her simultaneously. It was a bizarre image. She was facing the corner; with her back to me... she had been wiping down the sink. She stood stiff as a rail, awkwardly, if not painfully, so. She almost shivered and convulsed against her will. The mirror revealed her neck bulging with strained muscles, and her jaw was clamped shut. My gut reacted with the... wrongness... of the moment.

She had not spoken my name, I realized.

I stared more closely at her reflection in the mirror. She was absolutely terrified of something. Suddenly something moved in the mirror... a person swiftly shot by the doorway into the bedroom. I only got a glimpse, but that glimpse was enough. I saw only long skirts and a dark dress. I knew who it was instantly.

Rose. *Dead* Rose.

Though I had first encountered Rose near Room 8,

she had apparently resided in Room 4 all along. That was the only place people seemed to encounter her, anyway. I had always paid special attention to this room, originally built in 1859, in the hopes of experiencing what I just did. I stiffened just like Tina!

We both endured another agonizing moment of icy fear. Then I heard it again.

"Viki…" the whisper came. I reacted, as did Tina. It wasn't just my imagination! I wanted to bolt from the room, to flee as fast as I could. But I knew the only way out of the bathroom was through the bedroom of Room 4.

Past Rose.

"If she even knows your name," Tina blurted, coming alive, "I'm getting out of here!"

We both fled the scene as fast as we could. Now I avoid Room 4 at all costs.

***

I was making the bed in Room 5 one morning, doing my usual room cleanings. The sunrise from these two old rooms, Four and Five, are just spectacular. The sunlight was so intense, and it was just streaming through the glass door to the porch onto the bed. The frilly, translucent curtains were fluttering slightly with my hurried activities, so the patterns on the bed were dancing between brilliant sunlight and partial shadows. I was aggressively handling all my duties, when something made me pause at the bed.

Above the pillows, which I had finally set aright, was an inexplicable fuzziness. I stood at the foot of the bed, in front of the large mirror and dressing table there, and stared. Something above those pillows was just not right, but I couldn't place it. The sun hammered into me, and I began to sweat from my intense actions combined with the heat of the radiant summer morning.

Slowly the fuzziness began to take on some sort of form. It was so faint at first, but I realized relatively soon after it began coalescing that it was a face that I was looking at... a human face. I blinked in surprise. There was no fear, just plain surprise.

Now the face was truly taking on the full clarity of a regular object. The head of a man was rising out of the pillows. It was not a disembodied head floating there or anything like that. Slowly, as slowly as the face formed in the first place, the figure rose straight up and out of the bed... as if the bed were not there at all.

He wore a dark, old broken hat. It was of the wide brim, common style you see among 1870's period clothing. It had some faint stains on it, and appeared to have been well worn. His hair beneath was dark and thick, like his complete beard and long, substantial mustaches. Very curly and thick... and unkempt, as if he had not trimmed them in a long while. He continued to rise up and out of the bed, with a bland expression on his heavily lined face. He roughly faced me, but did not appear to notice me at all.

The sunlight struck him full upon his features as he continued to rise from the bed, illuminating more details about his appearance. A black suit jacket covered his slender shoulders. The seams were rough... they appeared to have been repaired by hand. The heavy sunlight revealed patches of thin material, where the well-worn coat had seen plenty of use. His white shirt was of a thick material, and possessed a short, bent collar.

The figure rose straight up and out of the bed to about his waist. Had the bed not been present at all, I suspect it would have been the equivalent of his standing there. He was not a large man, smaller than average, in fact. He stood motionless, not five feet before me, with the sunlight and shadows playing their games on his features… just like the bed he was standing *through*.

This, I realized, was the figure people had claimed to feel sitting at the foot of the bed when they are sleeping at night. Perhaps he was the one who shakes the beds, frightening the wits out of some people. I had plenty of time to study his features in the bright light of the morning. An odor emanated from him… as thick and intense as his mustaches… cigar smoke. Dense, heavy tobacco… not a cigarette, or even a sweet little cigar, but a real, heavy cigar. Now, this room was above the Great Room… but who would smoke a cigar this early? Besides, we didn't sell cigars at the Gold Hill Hotel… they would have to have been brought in by a smoker. It was not likely.

Then he was gone.

He just vanished, as if he had never been there. The cigar stench fled, too. No windows open at all… the smell came and went with the figure.

I was so surprised at the encounter, and so previously focused on work, I can honestly say I was not frightened. There was so much sunlight streaming in on the warm, comforting summer morning. Still, I *did* decide to finish this room later!

***

I had just exited one of the rooms in the new section of the hotel, and was absent-mindedly walking back to the front desk. It was a summer morning, and had been a busy one already, even though it was only mid-morning. I was wearing headphones and listening to music as I hopped from room to room, giving them the final check. Singing quietly to myself, I strode past a gentleman between Rooms 6 and 7.

"Hi, William," I called aloud, absent-mindedly.

The man turned with some fleeting surprise, then smiled genuinely at me. His teeth were straight, but they were darkly stained. He was not a tall man, with narrow shoulders and a thick black beard with huge, unkempt mustaches. I caught all these details as I was turning back to view where I was going, as I had not slowed.

Realization suddenly struck me, and I jerked my head back just as I turned the corner. There was no one else in the hall behind me. The doors to all the rooms were open, but I did not slow at all from getting out of the hallway… and certainly wasn't going to check each room!

Around the corner I let out a scream to relieve the sudden fright that shot through me at this casual and close encounter with a ghost. To my embarrassment, I nearly ran into a lady there, and I screamed right in her face. I had not heard her presence with my headphones on so loudly.

I can only wonder if William had actually said anything *back* to me.

***

"We used to have children [ghosts] that would play games. They loved to play with the cash register... and at the end of the night sometimes we would have this weird number [on it].... Or else they would sit on the couch... they used to sit with Carol. They would knock the arm covers off the couch or a chair on purpose... while she was sitting there. She'd put it back up and they pull it back down. And they used to like to go around and hit her [on her waist] where they could reach.

"We've seen little heads be-bop around. They haven't been around [lately], either. Maybe they found a happy place. The little girl would sit down on the stairs in the Great Room. She had a long blue dress with a white pinafore, and her hair was long and she had a big bow in the back of it. And the two little boys had the little short pants and little shirts... one had dark hair and one had blond hair. One was ... five and the other one six.

"One time Brandy and I were cleaning the rooms and we went down the hall, and were going down the stairs and we heard these little kids going, 'Nah nah nyah nah nah!' And they were looking through the rails at us. And the kids used to like to hide in Room 11."

***

Robin and I were cleaning Room 11 together one day. It was during the summer, so we had a lot of work to do that day… tourists were all over the place. The hotel was booked again tonight, so we had plenty to do with just cleaning the rooms. We were rushing about, but working well together. In record time we replaced and folded all the sheets. As she was finishing with the many pillows, I went to clean the bathroom. I was surprised to find the door locked from the inside.

I was positive the room's previous occupants had left for the morning, so I didn't hesitate at all to try and open the bathroom door. I jerked the doorknob, tried pushing it as I turned… all of the obvious techniques for opening a closed door. Nothing worked.

"Robin," I called to her as she slammed a pillow onto the bed. "Do you know how to open this door if it's locked from the inside?"

Without responding, she strode over to me with a second pillow in her hand. She reached past me and gently turned the doorknob. The door opened without hesitation, revealing the darkened interior of the bathroom. Frowning, I closed the door, listened to it latch, then tried to open it again. The knob resisted my attempt.

I glanced over to Robin. "Your turn again."

Once again, she reached past me and turned the knob smoothly. She pushed the door open.

My shoulders dropped. "What are you doing?"

She shrugged. "Nothing. It's not locked."

A third time I tried the door, but it refused to allow my entrance.

"Robin, this is weird. It will not open for me."

"Are you pushing in when you turn?" she suggested.

"No. Well, I can't even if I try… it just won't allow me to mess with it. Here, open the door once more."

Robin stepped back and tossed the pillow onto the

freshly made bed. Returning, she reached for the door, and I observed intently her action. The room was in the new section of the hotel... it was not an old door *or* lock. The clean white painted door appeared so normal and innocent in the bright, summer morning light. The knob, brass and tarnished on the sides from all the use of hands, was equally non-culpable. Like any other unlocked door, Robin turned the knob smoothly and pushed the door open to the dark little bathroom. As the door opened, I heard a faint sigh... almost as if the air pressure or wind had shifted inside the bathroom. There is, however, no window in this bathroom... and certainly no heat was pumping through the ventilation system. I jumped on this latest observation.

"Robin, listen for a second as I try. Tell me if you hear anything."

I pulled the door closed slowly until it clicked. We both leaned closely into the door as I gingerly grasped the knob. Just before my fingers closed around it, we both heard a faint whoosh, like wind being sucked into something. We stared at each other in mutual surprise. It felt like someone holding her breath in anticipation of something. Needless to say, I could not open the door. When Robin touched the handle, the faint sigh could be barely discerned inside the bathroom once again.

Richard, the maintenance man, gazed down in puzzlement at the doorknob. The bathroom refused entry for him, as well. We had wasted little more time with the problem after we called for Richard. There was just too much to do. And yet, now that we had third-party confirmation of the strange encounter, Robin and I let some of our duties slide for the time being.

"Did you hear the faint sound of wind?" Robin asked

him. He nodded in confusion. He gestured to Robin, who promptly opened the door. Immediately he stepped into the doorway and dropped to a knee. He studied the locking mechanism for the door, and played a bit with turning the knob on both sides of the door. The bolt moved smoothly outward, then retracted appropriately into its home in the door. He shook his head.

"Let me take it apart and see what's the matter with it." He immediately began reaching into his tool belt for the appropriate equipment. His eyes studied the lock intensely, probing for any obvious malfunction.

"Do you think it's the kids?" I blurted.

They both stopped and looked blandly at me.

"The kids?" Richard asked, confused. Robin gave me a sour, but knowing look. She knew exactly whom I was referring to.

"The ghost kids. The two boys. They like to play pranks."

Richard sighed. "Whatever. I'll just take it apart and have a look, OK?"

I shrugged indifferently. "Fine. We have plenty to do anyway. But you can't tell me that you didn't hear the swoosh wind when you grabbed the knob. The same thing happened to me. But Robin… it's different for her."

He didn't respond. Eventually Richard took the lock apart and found nothing out of the ordinary. He even took it to the locksmith that day… but everything was functioning properly. The locksmith had no explanation. Richard replaced the lock with a different model… one that allows locking and unlocking from *both* sides, if need be.

***

"They do tend to hide things. I remember once we had lost the… keys to open up all the doors on the property and we found them eventually in the oven downstairs in the kitchen… way in the *back* of the oven. Who would put them there?"

***

It was late on a winter night. The Washoe Zephyr was shrieking around the building as usual, and as I walked the corridor near the old rooms I could feel the structure shudder occasionally. The wind had a peculiar way of whistling through the bathroom window of Room 5. I had left the window cracked earlier, and now that it was late, I needed to lock the rooms down for the night.

The bedroom door was open, and I quickly swung through the very chilled chamber and entered the bathroom. It was very cold in the room, and I realized I should not have left it open for so long. I hurriedly closed the window, and took a quick peek outside. A mid-size car was scrunching through the freshly fallen snow, leaving four zigzagging trails as it turned around awkwardly in the narrow lot. The hill was very steep on the south side of the building, and the car slid sideways a bit as it exited. The night had long since fallen, but the snow retained a luminous glow from the bright and mostly full moon above. It was a crisp, clear night, and the stars throbbed above.

As I exited the room I snatched up a magazine that had been left on the nightstand. I casually perused the material as I slowly strode back to the front desk. The only sounds now came from the restaurant downstairs, which was quite full. I absent-mindedly locked all the doors as I passed, as no one was staying in the hotel this night. I didn't want any of the bar-crowd to enter the rooms after I left.

Something made me pause. There was a sound that seemed faint but out of place. I realized it came from above me, and not below. I had already locked all the rooms upstairs, about an hour ago in fact. But there was some sort of commotion faintly emanating from the stairs. I stood at the base of the stairs and glanced up past the landing of the stairwell. All the lights up there were supposed to be off, but the hall light was still on. Obviously I had overlooked the main hall light. Still, there were many sounds dropping down the stairwell.

Placing the magazine under my arm, I labored up the steps. It had been a long, tiring day, and I could feel my body resisting any further trials. Once I made the landing, however, I stopped cold. There was a lot of sound coming from upstairs… a loud ruckus almost, as if an entire party was in full swing. Once up the stairs, I swallowed a quickly rising knot in my throat. My breathing quickened a bit, for I knew something was not right.

The two visible doors were wide open, and light streamed into the hallway from inside the rooms. The noise was very loud, and I recognized a news channel from a TV set. I had personally locked up all the rooms, and they had been all dark and quiet. I was the only person with all the keys at this point in the night.

I hesitantly approached the first open door. It was

obvious the TV was on in the room, and also obviously turned with volume at full. It sounded like the radio was maximized as well. I entered the chamber and noted all of the lights were on: the bathroom lights, the bedroom lights, and the nightlights… the TV was on, as was the clock-radio, which was blaring some static from a poorly received station.

This was weird. I felt very uncomfortable as I entered the room. I snapped off the nearest wall sconce. Then the next. I had to reach around and turn off the radio. I lowered the volume after it was off. I hesitantly went over to the TV and did the same. I clicked off the nightlight. In the bathroom I flicked off a number of switches, too. I had the strangest feeling they would all start to turn on again behind my back, one after another. I envisioned the sound of the TV turning itself on and blaring at me so clearly that I almost jumped at nothing.

I hurriedly closed and locked the door to the now darkened room behind me, and made my way to the next room.

This room, too, was fully exposed and pulsing with electricity. The TV was still turned to full volume, and was surprisingly on the same news channel as the previous set. Once again I turned everything off, and the feeling it would all start up again right in my presence was unnerving. I was jittery, I realized. The slightest thing would make me jump. Steeling myself, I made my way down the hall.

I stopped at the corner of the hallway, and looked behind me. I really, really was uncomfortable with this… thing… behind me. But I had to do what I had to do. I turned the corner and faced the next few rooms, all of which demonstrated the same behavior. All the lights

were on. All the radios were on, and all the televisions were blaring at full volume the local news channel.

I fairly ran through the rooms to turn everything off. I was not happy about going to the end of the hallway that had obviously been under the influence of… something. Once all the rooms had been dealt with, I strode hurriedly back towards the stairs leading down. I could hear, however, the sound of the news again. It was coming from where I had already been. I turned the corner, and my heart dropped as I saw the door to the first room fully open, with light streaming into the hall!

**Mark Twain began his writing
career as a reporter in Virginia City
for the Territorial Enterprise.**

THE HISTORY

While the exact date of construction for the Gold Hill Hotel remains unknown, it is generally believed to have been built in 1859. The structure apparently began as 'The Reisen House', and is shown definitively in an 1862 photograph revealing repairs to its south side following the previous year's floods. "...the southwest and southeast corners of the Risen (sic) House, a fine structure, have fallen, but the main part of the building remained firm."$_{(1)}$ The southern structure was replaced, but was eventually lost again sometime in the 1890s.

Within a few years the building became known as Vesey's Hotel, named after its new owner, H.M. Vesey. It was by this name the structure was known through the heady days of the Comstock. The early 1950s, when the city's population was less than eighty people, saw the renaming of the property to its current name. The Crown Point Restaurant and additional rooms were added in the mid-1980s. The Gold Hill Hotel is the oldest continually running hotel in Nevada. $_{(2)}$

January 8th, 1859 saw the beginnings of the famous Comstock Lode discovered just above the site of Vesey's Hotel. The Sierra Nevada gave up enough gold and silver to support the united metropolis of Gold Hill, Silver City, and Virginia City. The combined populations of the area rapidly rose to greater than 40,000 souls. Vesey's Hotel, being centrally located, held an important role in the boom times, providing lodging, a banquet hall, and saloon. Eventually the Yellow Jacket mine's hoisting works dominated the hill above the hotel, and the building became a miner's bunkhouse. $_{(3)}$

48

THE YELLOW JACKET CATASTROPHE

"...about three o'clock in the morning a second fire and series of explosions occurred in the Yellow Jacket mine, by which six men lost their lives and several were seriously injured (Dan DeQuille, *The Big Bonanza*)."

The hills surrounding the Gold Hill Hotel are filled with the abandoned tunnels and silent shafts of numerous such mines as the Yellow Jacket. It was not uncommon for fires to blaze an unstoppable swath of destruction and death through these mines. One such fire, that of the 20th of September 1873, ripped through the Yellow Jacket mine, killing dozens of unfortunate miners before it was contained. An explosion shook the very stone of the mountain, and flames shot as far as the Belcher mine, thousands of feet away. Men who were in the Crown Point mine stated the fire "seemed a solid mass that filled all the space about them and that it flashed toward and past them as swiftly as lightning. At the same time the concussion that accompanied the flash was so great as to knock them down and drive them along the ground for a considerable distance." (4)

The twisted remains of the Yellow Jacket mine awkwardly protrude from the sandy hill upon which the hotel is perched. Just a few dozen yards from the Crown Point restaurant is the Changing Room and the hoisting head frame from the mine, among other broken relics from the past. Indeed, a nearby shaft bores thousands of feet into the earth, barely a hundred feet from the rooms.

WORKS CITED

1. Territorial Enterprise of January 13th, 1862
2. The Gold Hill Hotel Information Booklet
3. The Gold Hill Hotel, A Country Inn, Brochure
4. The Big Bonanza, pp.132-133

Silver Kings John Mackay and Jack O'Brien first crossed the Sierra on foot with only 50 cents between them... and they threw it away.

THE HUNT

I'm not exactly sure what I expected when I stayed at the Gold Hill Hotel, but it most certainly was *not* what I encountered. This vigil was special because it was my first ghost hunt. I was not really sure what I should bring. In hindsight, I should have brought a bouquet of flowers and chocolates.

I arrived at Room 4, or Rose's Room, at a little past 9:00 PM on the night of Wednesday, November 14th (Rose is the name of the ghost who currently resides here... no foreshadowing at all). I had with me little more than my gym bag filled with a change of clothing and perhaps some vague hopes for an encounter with the supernatural. The door was open and waiting for me, and I crossed the threshold from the 21st century back into the 19th.

The room was lovely. It was pink, but still quite lovely nonetheless. A small room of perhaps twelve feet square, it was dominated by a large four-poster bed, complete with canopy and a flowery comforter that matched the throw pillows that were, well, thrown about. Immediately upon entering I nearly smacked my head into a floral-patterned lamp that thrust itself out from the wall. The whole feeling was of lovely, Victorian charm. The furniture was period, though admittedly I am only surmising the period was Victorian. The wood was all old, polished and lovely.

Did I mention the room was lovely? In my dictation of that night I used the word lovely no less than five times. Either my vocabulary had fled at the thought of a ghostly encounter, or the room was... lovely. The porch outside afforded absolutely phenomenal views of sunsets over the rugged and beautiful sage-shrouded Sierra Nevada Mountains... it was romantic in the extreme. Little did I know how much love was in the air.

I knew from previous inquiries there was a ghost that dwelt here. People called her Rose, and many, many had seen her. Guests with no forewarning had approached the hotel staff the next morning and informed them of restless spirits in the rooms... sometimes even of conversations with them! Rose was usually identified by an inexplicable and strong smell of roses in the air... hence her name, apparently. The scent of her 'perfume', as many like to call it, comes and goes without rhyme or reason.

There was little or no sound coming from elsewhere in the hotel, as a play was currently unfolding in the Great Room and bar below me. I strode about the room and began dictating my thoughts. The room was pink (and lovely), and quite old. There was an eight-foot window facing the north, and a glass door leading to the porch on the east side of the building, overlooking the Sierra. The corners around these features were bereft of plaster, having long ago roughly broken off to reveal the old brickwork beneath. This, too, was painted pink, and it all seemed to fit nicely, partially hidden as it was behind flowery, sheer curtains.

I held my tape recorder before me and ran a quick test on a new tape. I narrated flatly for perhaps twenty to twenty-five seconds, "This is a test, the microphone is about three feet away from me as I speak in this average voice... average for me but loud enough to wake the dead for anyone else...the volume is at max...", etc. I viewed the artwork on the walls as I listened to the test with dissatisfaction. I rewound the tape and lowered the volume aggressively, hoping for a less garbled sound.

Before I blandly blurted out the usual testing words, I stared at a work of art on the wall. It was a cupid picture presented in an old, sepia-toned style... a photograph of a little girl perhaps four years old. She was naked from the waist up, and all around were heavy, dark, soft shadows. She held a bow and arrow over and behind her head, and did not appear as a cutesy-Raphaelesque angel at all. She had a big head of blond curls, and eyes that stared intently at me... *very* intently at me.

I moved closer. Those eyes had something far more interesting in them than just a four-year-old's knowledge. I started the next dictation test and locked eyes with the cupid. There was something in those eyes all right, but I didn't know what. The picture jerked itself awkwardly on the wall as I continued with my narration, but I just continued watching it until my test was complete.

I leaned close to the wall and studied the artwork. The frame was a darkly stained wooden surface cut into a heart-shape on the inside, so it needed no matting to couch the art in that romantic shape. It had previously been hanging level upon the wall, but had moved *itself* somewhat sideways. Admittedly the wall was anything but flat: it was unevenly plastered, with swirls and plenty of character. There were patches and big, thick lumps beneath the pink paint, and the entire surface was visibly bowed with age. I dismissed the odd occurrence and listened to my test.

Clearly I could hear, "This is the next test...," but then there was a distinct click. It sounded exactly as if I had pressed the stop button. I know I had spoken for at least twenty seconds, and remember clearly pressing the stop button at the end of my test. But what I heard next sent a jolt of electricity through me. Stunned, I hurriedly rewound the tape to the beginning (only about three seconds away) and listened to the strange, inexplicable sound again.

"This is the next test....Click!.... ooouuhh...."

There it was again! There was absolutely no denying it: there was a recording of a woman moaning... in pleasure. It was not a muffled blurb or word or anything... it was exactly that... a moan of passion and bliss. It was way too breathy and heavy to be anything else. This was not some ghostly, haunted moan of eternal unrest... this was the *very* warm, *very* recognizable sound of a woman in sexual pleasure...

...coinciding *exactly* when the cupid's picture moved inexplicably on the wall.

I shot my head up to look back at the cupid. She was boring those eyes into me still. That was no four-year old! What was going on in those eyes?

I rewound the tape and listened to it again. Directly after the unmistakable moaning my previous recording started up again. My half-minute, last test had been cut off abruptly at merely five seconds. What else could it be? I scrupulously studied that sound over and over. Ooouuhh... ooouuhh...OOOUUHH!

How could this be? I had heard nothing as I narrated. The play was commencing downstairs so quietly I heard nothing from them... no sounds…no wind. Unfortunately, no women in the room, either.

Except one. Rose.

I sat down in shock. Rose was speaking to me through the cupid picture. What was she trying to say? What else? She liked me. She wanted me. Rose, the non-living tenant of Gold Hill Hotel for nearly a century and a half had the hots for me. I was occasionally loud enough to wake the dead... but I never knew I was attractive enough to *arouse* the dead! I sat up a little taller on the bed, and smoothed my sweater a bit. I guess if you've got it, you've got it. This encounter happened at 9:22 PM.

Still somewhat stunned, I arose and dictated my thoughts on the (lovely) room. It very much had the feel of a romantic place, with the warmth of the pink walls, and the Victorian décor. The canopy was sheer enough that a soft, white glow permeated beneath the bed. This was an ideal room for a private getaway. Did I really want to spend the night in this romantic place with a ghost who was sexually attracted to me?

Shaking off the thought, I went into the bathroom. There was a four-inch step to gain access into the bathroom, which I had been informed was originally the public toilet for the whole hotel. Now, however, it was only for Rose's room. The doorknob was oddly low, revealing the ancient roots of this place even more than the only 6'2" high doorway. It was fortunate I had to reach down for the knob, as I am nearly 6'2" myself.

The bathroom floor was of very old stone. It was vaguely smoothed by over a century of use, with big round stones set into the floor. The walls were painted white, with a four-foot wainscoting of highly polished, dark wood. One corner was dominated by a big brick protuberance, which I speculated was a chimney from a hearth below. There was one large window facing north and offering a view of the hotel's entrance, and a big bathtub surrounded on all sides by wooden planks. The art on the wall showed two naked children before a hearth.

I slowly undressed and started running the water,

though my mind was on the recording. What do you do with a 140-year old woman who wants to get close to you in such an incredibly romantic (and lovely) place? How can you tell her, 'sorry, I have a headache tonight?' She is everywhere... you can't just roll over and turn your back to her. She was everywhere, seeing everything. I began to feel self-conscious. This was *her* domain, *her* haunt. And I... I was getting naked.

Was she seeing this? Was she ogling my nude body, even as I thought about it? I was becoming extremely uncomfortable. I was being viewed... I *knew* there were eyes on my body. Did she think I looked good? *Did* I look good? Why else would she moan with such pleasure, and the image of the cupid shiver? The hair crept up slowly on the back of my neck as I felt eyes scanning every inch of my body. What was I, a piece of meat? I was being violated! I was... I was... I was standing naked in front of an open eight-foot window.

Sheepishly, I hurriedly closed the pink, floral-patterned drapes that hid my presence from the deck in front of the hotel... where there were people outside congregating. Perhaps I was over-reacting. Sounds of revelry from outside and in the bar below drifted up as the play ended. Embarrassed with myself, I knew the laughter was not directed at me, but I couldn't help but feel it was.

To ease my chagrin, I enjoyed a steaming bath, then threw myself onto the bed. I was very fatigued, and I instantly fell asleep in my towel. After an hour I awoke to a stifling silence. The bar obviously closed down, and I was now the only person in the building. I had been informed of this during my checking in... should I need anything, there was no one to help me. Silence. It was so painfully silent I could hear the sound of blood pumping in my head. I almost would have preferred the wind to whistle around the porch like it had earlier in the evening, sighing through the railings.

I read a book until around midnight, then slipped into the bed. I stared up at the warm, glowing canopy above me. I suddenly realized I had not brought my glasses. Sigh. What kind of ghost hunter am I? I have poor enough hearing (perhaps explaining why I speak so loudly), my eyesight was pathetic without my glasses or contact lenses… and I had absolutely no sense of smell to speak of. What kind of sensory arsenal did this leave me with? Taste? I had serious doubts about my being able to identify a soul that has defied death for over one hundred and forty years with my tongue. And touch?

I swallowed the uncomfortable thought. Would I be able to identify Rose by touch? Ordinarily the thought of my actual, physical contact with a ghost would be, well, not entirely pleasant. But Rose…she *wanted* to touch me. And here I was, lying naked in her bed. What kind of message was I sending? Should I not sleep in the nude, as I usually do? What if something freaks me out, and I go running into the frigid foothills of the Sierra, naked? I only had dress pants with me, however, and did not relish the thought of sleeping in those. I already had to sleep in my contact lenses, however. After all, I wanted to see whatever was there to be seen.

I lay in bed and pondered such things. Time ticked by, very slowly. I wasn't sure if the light should stay on or off. I resolved on for tonight, and off for the next visit of mine to this hotel (Room #5 was also supposedly haunted, and I was booked for that one, too). As time drug on, I stared at the canopy above. I heard nothing but my own blood pumping. Several hours passed in this uncomfortable fashion.

I began wondering what Rose looked like. Was she attractive... even if in some out-dated kind of way? With my contacts drying up and burning in my eyes I should be able to see her. Was she too old for me? It was getting stuffy in the room, but my skin was clammy. Would I feel her touch as cold? What would I do if she slipped into bed beside me? As boastful as men tend to be about the number and variety of women they have known, did I really want to top everyone else's stories with *this*? I wasn't sure if I wanted to go where no man had gone before.

I lay there, with my head swallowed by the massive feathered pillows. I tried to sleep, but only grudgingly did my eyes close. This was in part due to my contacts, which I have trained myself to not sleep in. I finally found myself drifting off to sleep.

What was that? I was instantly alert. I remained in the bed, motionless. My fiery eyes scanned the room, and I strained for another sound... but there was nothing. I probably heard nothing at all, but my heightened awareness picked it up. This was a building over a century old... and not exactly built to last. Of course it was going to make a few sounds at night. I tried to mentally relax and resume sleep. This pathetic sequence of events continued for hours.

Around 5:00 AM I finally fell into a real sleep, which was not disturbed until morning. The sunlight hammered into me through the glass door leading to the east porch. I achingly and grudgingly arose from bed and took a look around. There were no signs of nocturnal spiritual activity. What was I expecting? Did I think she was going to pass me a secret note, like children in school? I readied myself for work and enjoyed the brilliant sunrise. My morning routine is very fast and efficient, and within a few minutes I was ready to reenter the modern world.

My eyes dropped to the chocolate mints on the nightstand just as I opened the door to leave.

"Rose, my dear," I called aloud in the room, "you can have the chocolates. I can only apologize for not bringing some flowers. You have such a lovely room!"

The Pony Express ran through Nevada (just south of Virginia City) between April 1860 and October 1861.

III

SILVER TERRACE CEMETERY

**Mine shaft temperatures rose five
degrees for every one hundred feet
they descended.**

"At one time [the] cemeteries reflected Virginia City in its heyday. The local newspapers noted elaborate monuments, iron and picket fences, graveled walks and carriageways. The landscape was thriving with trees, and flowering plants such as morning glories, rose bushes and thick carpets of clover. Much has changed since those days...as you walk these grounds you will no doubt become aware of the toll vandalism and the ravages of time have taken on the cemetery. Modern day burials are still occurring within the Silver Terrace Cemeteries." (The Silver Terrace Cemeteries Brochure)

The *Comstock Cemetery Foundation* [(775) 847-0281] hosts daily tours of the Silver Terrace Cemetery, and distributes a newsletter on its activities twice each year. It also graciously accepts sponsors of unknown or unmarked sites.

The Hauntings

I used to enjoy wandering at night. Virginia City after dark is a step back into another time and another world. The tourists all have either left, or have settled in for the night, leaving the streets sadly empty. The pale yellow light from the gas lamps combats the silver moonlight on the boardwalk, and the facades of all the old buildings take on a decrepit, washed-out look. The wind always whips over the quiet streets and pushes at the wooden business signs, which creak back and forth on old chains. You can hear coyotes in the dark hours… it is all you would expect from a ghost town… only this one struggles to maintain life.

So in the late hours of the day, or even the early hours of the morning, I have been known to wander through the debris-filled lanes of the old cemetery. The views from the hill are impressive in the moonlight, and on a clear night the valleys are visible for a long, long way off. Usually I am alone on these walks, just sucking up the atmosphere and getting a feel for the place.

One summer night I was in the graveyard, on the southern slope of the big hill. It was a pretty dark night, and I needed my flashlight to avoid stepping on any broken wooden rails or into unmarked graves. A noise caught my ear, and I stopped instantly. I heard a grating sound, specifically, like stone sliding on concrete. The acoustics of the hillside are weird, so I had to wander for a bit to find the source. I didn't know what it was from the sound of it, but it was pretty loud in the quiet night.

My flashlight sliced through the dark, back and forth, but finally fell upon a moderately sized marble headstone.

It was a new or refurbished stone in great condition. Below it, resting on the concrete base, was a large stone bowl about eight inches in diameter and twelve inches deep. The ornate sides were molded to resemble handles, and the interior was filled with cheap plastic flowers. They were very dirty, and had bits of broken tumbleweed stuck among their petals. The bowl was the source of the sound.

This bowl, before my very eyes, was slowly rotating on the rim of its base. It had a strong angle as it spun about... an angle close to forcing it over onto its side for good. But it did not fall over... it just slowly rotated along its rim, oblivious to me. The flowers tumbled about as it churned around.

After a few full rotations, the heavy concrete bowl came to rest solidly upon its base once again, and the night grew quiet. With wide eyes, I came a bit closer and studied the scene with more detail. The grave was an old one, with an occupant who had died in 1874, aged thirty-eight years. It was a refurbished headstone, then. The tombstone rose out of the dry ground, resting on a concrete base.

The bowl itself was of course concrete, like any common lawn ornament. I leaned closer and let my light fall upon it. Dirt filled the many pockmarks in its sides, and all the creases of the plastic flower petals were caked with it. I leaned over to view the depths of the bowl, past the plastic flowers. Just before my eyes caught sight of the bottom, the entire bowl suddenly rose up on one side, and started slowly rotating once more... mere inches from me! I left the bowl to itself, stomped away, and let the sound of grinding stone fade away into the darkness behind me.

***

Another night when I was wandering in the cemetery, I saw something else unusual. Once again, I was wandering about in silent contemplation. This was in the fall, and the weather was pretty chilly. I had on a heavy coat and gloves, but had sincerely wished for a scarf as well. The winds were particularly chill that night, and pushed me around with much strength.

A light moved behind me, and I whirled about to see who else was in the cemetery. Needless to say, not many people hang out in the cemetery after dark, but there are a few of us who enjoy doing so. I would imagine it is more popular than many modern cemeteries for this type of behavior, due to its age. The light flashed between the tombstones, flaring brilliantly one second, and then disappearing behind the black outline of a grave the next. My eyes darted about, seeking the source, and was surprised to see two children running among the headstones.

I called out to them, but they did not answer. In my brief glimpses I recognized a boy and a girl, both about ten years old. They were wearing pretty worn clothing... the boy in a red shirt and the girl in a tattered blue dress. I am not sure about the girl, as it was dark and I only got a glimpse of her. I saw the boy more clearly, because he was the one holding the light. It was an old-style *lantern*, of all things. Regardless, they weren't wearing enough... it was way too cold for them to be in such light clothing.

I followed them, more to give them a piece of my mind than anything else. It was legal to be in the cemetery at night in those days (unlike the present), but that didn't mean kids should be running around like that.

They ran around a corner, and the light began to fade behind an old, gnarled pine tree and a massive manzanita plant. A broken rail tried to fence off the corner. I stepped around the obstacles and flashed my light around. I couldn't see their light any more, but I could tell from the lay of the hillside they were nearby and not around another corner. They obviously thought this was a game, and had smothered their light.

I called out that I was in no mood for games, and continued searching for them. There was nothing but the wind and my shouting. I looked down to see if there were any footprints or anything, but was not particularly successful. I'm not a tracker, after all, and it wasn't muddy out, or I wouldn't have been there. But then something near the ground caught my eye.

There were two old, wooden headstones half buried under some scrubby plants. The letters, which had been carved in so long ago, were splintered and difficult to read, and had blackened with age. I could barely make them out. It was the grave of a brother and sister, both of whom died at age nine... over one hundred years ago.

That was the last time I went into the cemetery after dark.

***

"It's common knowledge that a tombstone glows at night. Not every time, of course, but I can think of a dozen people who've seen it... at *least*. Especially from the RV park near there... a lot of people claim to see it who don't even live here. You can see it from C Street, too."

THE HISTORY

The area of and around Flowery Hill, the home of the Silver Terrace Cemeteries, actually contains a total of thirteen separate entities. These are as follows: the Masonic, the Oddfellows, the Pioneer, the Vault, the Silver Terrace, the West End, The Firemen's, the Wilson and Brown, the Order of Redmen, the Knights of Pythias, St. Mary's Catholic, and the city and county cemeteries. (1)

Isaac B. Wollard, a successful entrepreneur who built a toll bridge on the Carson River among other ventures, authored the petition to create the county cemetery. In 1863 his petition, specifically asking for a portion of the County Hospital land to be set aside for the cemetery, was passed.

The seventy-two acres of given land had first been surveyed in 1862, and were entirely within the corporate limits of Virginia City. The rapid growth of the city catalyzed the Board of Aldermen in 1863 to not allow any more burials within the city limits. The unpleasant task of moving all those buried to a new location was given to Wollard. He removed one hundred forty males, nineteen females, and forty-four children from the earth, and moved them to the new Flowery Hill Cemetery.

Even though the new Flowery Hill Cemetery was laid out in sections, plots, and streets, by the end of the year most of the mounds of earth still did not have markers. A local paper viciously commented upon this disrespect. "We cannot believe that the eager pursuit of wealth, the greed for gain, has so absorbed the thoughts of the living among us that they forget the dead as soon as they are placed in the sod. Why is it that scarce a grave in the Territory has been adorned with a monument?" (2)

Another example of this lack of attention relates to none other than Captain Storey, for whom the entire county is named. Killed in the Paiute War of 1860, he was buried in the Silver Terrace Cemetery. However, seventeen years later in 1877, his grave was still unmarked. No stone at all was placed upon his grave until 1879, when a friend purchased a small slab. This marker was broken, lost, and not rediscovered until 1913. Only in 1930, seventy years after his death, was Captain Storey's grave graced with a headstone.

THE BURIAL VAULT

During the Comstock days, there was but a single vault in all of Nevada, or so bragged undertaker Brown in 1874 to two newspapermen. It was built in the cut originally made for a proposed Sierra Nevada Railroad tunnel, which was to connect with the V&T short line. The journalists for the *Daily Independence* requested a visit to this vault. The undertaker agreed, and decided to play a prank upon the men.

"[We] had no sooner set foot inside the vault, when the doors were closed with a slam, the key turned in the lock, and we [were] left in total darkness, thirty or forty feet underground, with dead bodies for companions. Resistance being unavailing, we quietly submitted to our fate and having matches with us, proceeded to strike a light. Upon glancing around – not without trepidation – we saw some half a dozen iron caskets, of various sizes, bearing inscriptions stating the name, age, and time of death of the person whose remains were contained therein. We were about copying off the inscriptions, when the key turned in the lock and 'Cap' Brown made his appearance, explaining by way of apology that he expected the fright would kill us and he'd have the job of burying us." [3]

WORKS CITED

1. The Silver Terrace Cemeteries Brochure
2. Virginia Evening Bulletin, November 3, 1863
3. The History of Virginia City, NV Cemeteries, pp.1-5, 7-8, 18-19

The Pony Express route was about 2,000 miles long, and took about 10 days to travel. Horses were exchanged every 10-15 miles, and riders every 33.

THE HUNT

The night was black as can be. It was rare to have total cloud cover over Northern Nevada, but the night was doing its best to smother out any light, anywhere. The gas lamps of Virginia City teased the atmosphere in the distance, illuminating the steep slopes of Mt. Davidson and spilling loosely into Six Mile Canyon below. I trudged warily parallel to these lonely spots of the living. A wide graveled trail led up to the main gate of the Silver Terrace Cemetery.

My flashlight struck the ground before me. I concluded it was frightened of the night, as it refused to venture very far. A large brick and iron gate loomed up suddenly out of this darkness, and I paused to take in the situation. My flashlight was only strong enough to illuminate ten feet in front of me with any real authority. After that, the white light faded quickly when pummeled by the inky blackness that shrouded the cemetery. Sage silhouettes shivered just outside the beam, and beyond them was a slowly shifting blackness just a bit less black than the rest of the night.

Looking up at those gates… and the faintly visible movement beyond them… I realized I was actually somewhat nervous to enter. I almost expected the old gate to proclaim "Abandon Hope All Ye Who Enter Here." Even if I wasn't actually unnerved, I certainly felt my usual cheery attitude was unwelcome. A quick stroke of the light revealed tall, pale white obelisks rising out of the night, reaching past the low clusters of sage. From here the graveyard beyond appeared densely packed with the memorials to the dead.

Hefting my pack higher onto my shoulder, I waded into the sea of tombstones. This dead sea parted for me, but it churned and shifted restlessly just beyond the reach of my light, waiting to fill in and drown me. I immediately veered off the widest path and started into areas more tightly packed with residents. Generally I progressed uphill.

I jerked the light about furiously as I tried to see everything. I was completely surrounded by the dead. I would hear a sound, then snap my light onto it. After I realized it was nothing, I was loath turning the light away, since I had grown comfortable with a sight.

The trail inevitably pushed me higher and higher up the hill, and my progress was dominated by the magnificent presence of an obelisk at the brow of the hill. The trail began to narrow as it approached this pinnacle of majesty, and I was forced to labor up beneath its steady presence. The path was flanked with the twisted and blasted skeletal grasp of trees. Their pale fingers glowed as they dipped into the light.

Up on top of the hill I paused and viewed the entire cemetery. An undisciplined army of pale white tombstones stretched below me, the obelisks pointing skyward like pikes. My eyes slowly acclimated to the absence of natural light, and the yellow points to the south grew larger as I adjusted. Certain areas were black as pitch, however… usually in the lee of the hill, away from the city… away from the living.

I strode quietly and mindlessly along the paths, snaking my way down to the south. The hill was surprisingly steep and long, and the entire slope was littered with recognizable tombstones as well as the shattered wooden remains of the forgotten dead. Pinion pines broke the monotony of headstones, surprisingly lush and alive. I spent my energies on viewing the path, which was somewhat treacherous, and trying to avoid stepping on what appeared to be a grave itself. This, I knew, was pointless, as there could be any number of unknown burials here in the last tumultuous century.

Suddenly I stopped. Barely visible behind a jutting black silhouette of a tombstone, I saw a faintly glowing... something. I had heard the tales of the glowing headstone visible from town. Well, I was now on the south side of Flowery Hill, and therefore in line of sight of the city. And, sure enough, I moved over and saw a faint glow. It was not a tombstone glowing, however.

The glowing figure of a man lay before a tombstone.

I blinked in shock, and then snapped my flashlight towards it. It was too far away for my feeble light to add any illumination. I squinted, and studied the shape more intently. It was obviously a man, whose large belly was distinctly outlined by the blackness behind it. His feet stuck up as well, though his head was still a bit blurry from where I stood. Could I really believe this was a man... the *ghost* of a man?

After another few moments, with the figure still there, I resolved to take a closer look. I stepped forward, completely unafraid. I was an inspiration to any who would have seen me. It was one of those moments so eventful you wish someone else was nearby to share it... and also to verify that I was, in fact, completely unafraid. I desperately wished for third-party confirmation of my stalwart condition while it lasted. I would have photographed myself had there been more light.

I only needed another step or two to realize that it was not, in fact, the glowing figure of a man lying on top of a grave. It was a broken obelisk of a particularly clean, white marble. It *somehow* found enough light to reflect back at me. I was astounded... simply amazed, in fact. How could an obelisk break into such an uncanny resemblance to a fat man? Most *artists* aren't that convincing.

I scrunched away, shaking my head. An interesting encounter, but just barely.

The night progressed, and I went deeper and deeper into the cemetery. I avoided the main paths, and took pains to be near as many clusters of graves as I could. I had no particular reason why, but I did feel any encounter would be away from the main avenues. I stopped myself from humming and even whistling, as the awesome silence begged to be broken. I didn't want to come tramping in here... I wanted to be silent, smooth, and unobtrusive. Well, as unobtrusive as possible in a bright yellow ski jacket.

I found myself on a road, and followed it east, where it curved to reveal the Catholic section of the cemetery. It had its own gate: a thin, twisted metal sentry that faintly whistled as a breeze tickled its letters. A barbed wire fence surrounded the area, which was a large round knob, peaked with a very tall cross.

I entered and followed the path to about half way up the hill before turning right. The graves were of varying distances apart from each other, and I walked the line that abutted the barbed wire. A chill breeze had begun, and I shivered. One grave, I noted, was littered with oyster shells. Yes, oyster shells.

This gave me pause. Why would someone picnic here on oysters? Or was this the migratory destination of the extremely rare and unlikely Washoe Desert Clam? I doubted it… but what did I know?

A number of dogs barked in the city. Higher onto the hill I went, and the sound grew more distinct and audible. Likewise, the breeze strengthened. A scrambling sound caught my ear… movement. It sounded large. I froze and reviewed the radiating graves atop the shadowy summit of the hill. It could be a jackrabbit… most likely it was… but it sounded bigger. My mind refused to loose the mental image of a canine. A coyote, then… but where? This was the only place in the cemetery I could see enough from the natural light to make out anything as large as a coyote. But then, they are small animals, really.

I wandered around, and heard the sound again. Was that a low growl? No, it must have been the wind, which was getting pretty strong. Then I heard some scrambling… just like a dog clawing at a wooden door. It was uncanny… and it was right at my feet. Mildly alarmed, I looked down and blasted the area with the beam from my flashlight.

I stood before a small wooden tombstone. The wood, splintered and weathered, was fully intact. Piled around the base was a small rectangle of stones.

I saw nothing to account for the sound. It did not appear to emit from the tombstone itself. However, this area was definitely the source. What was causing this sound? I saw no movement, such as a rabbit in flight, but that didn't mean anything. My senses were as far from predatory as possible… only pizza need fear me. I stared at the grave, and listened again. Nothing. But the impression of a dog was stronger in my mind, and visions of Wile E. Coyote came to mind. Was I about to get hammered by an Acme Super Rocket Blaster? It was more probable than my being stampeded by a migrating herd of Washoe Desert Clams.

My pale white light had difficulty discerning the name on the wooden tombstone. B- something – R? – C – K – E. Burcke, it read. No, wait, it did not end in E, but I – E.

Burckie?

I frowned, and glanced closer. Below the name were additional letters, which were clearer. HOUND DOG. Hound dog? I started over again.

It was the grave of Blackie, the Hound Dog.

I stood there, with my shoulders slumped. No, this could not be. This was not the sound of Blackie, coming back from the dead. A good hound dog would stay with his master… no matter what, and not scramble at the grave holding him down.

Suddenly I was hammered by a burly blast of wind. I actually had to take a step back to brace myself. It was a powerful, unbroken push from the west. A mournful, deep whistling then surrounded me. This, I knew, was what everyone expects to hear in a cemetery! It was the unmistakable sound of the wind whispering between graves and sighing through the trees. I turned and feebly struck the tree with my light. It was far enough away that it only faintly was visible. It shrugged at me.

The scratching sound stopped, and I was buffeted again by the wind. It was not only a strong wind, but also very chill. I shivered, and trudged back to the main path. The wind followed me, jerking roughly at my collar. A massive pinion thrashed madly as I walked by, and I found myself leaning away from it. It was seething in the gale. It was almost absurd, but I felt it was trying to keep me away. I hunkered down into the force and passed through the Catholic gates.

The air stream was not quite as bad here, and I trudged

up the eastern slope of the main cemetery. Here the graves were sporadic, and the sage was large and completely dominant. This was the general vicinity of the Vault, I realized. I paused halfway up, and listened. I could hear many, many trees bucking and pitching in the winds. It howled through the canyons and ravines. I could feel the tension building, too. The storm was already strong enough to nearly knock over a large, metal 55-gallon trash bin… and it was getting stronger. This was powerful stuff indeed.

I finally topped the rise, and slipped through an opening in the barbed wire. As soon as the brow of the hill no longer protected me, the gust blasted mercilessly. I staggered back, amazed. Debris skittered over the rough ground, catching in the scrub, and then tearing violently away to continue its mad dash to the east. The immediate area had numerous pines, and they all whipped about me. I struggled up to the top of the hill and met up with that solitary, majestic obelisk that greets people on the path from the main gate. It stood strong and resolute against the incessant rush of the wind.

"You, my friend," I said, nodding to the grave, "are strong, indeed!"

I stumbled down to the north. I passed behind a series of what appeared to be manzanita in the dark, and was greeted with a stunning blow from the storm. The entire north slope was a wind tunnel, and it shrieked by with a violence actually frightening. I staggered into the air current, and dodged the vicious swinging branches of numerous trees. A large two-foot tumbleweed hurtled past me as if shot from a cannon.

This was becoming completely and utterly bizarre. I had not experienced winds like these since I was literally caught in a tornado! The roar of the wind, coupled with the snarling trees, deafened me. I saw the gate ahead of me, rocking back and forth… or was it *me* shaking like mad? The wooden slats of the gate were all flapping angrily and noisily at me. I leaned into the wind, and regarded once more the scene around me.

It was insane. Everything was moving… the trees growled at me, the gate snapped at me, and the wind ripped at me. The varying levels of blackness, as they progressed further and further from me, all seethed and boiled with rage. I don't know if any of it was directed at me, but it certainly felt that way! Hefting my pack once more, I stumbled out of the cemetery, weary and actually feeling beaten. I hurled myself into my Jeep, which rocked madly under the power of the storm. It shuddered so hard from one blast of wind I actually feared it would tip!

I pulled the Jeep around, and bullied my way out of the cemetery parking lot against the gusts. I was not sure what I felt… shock, mostly, at the surreal amount of wind that had popped up so suddenly.

I had entered the Silver Terrace Cemetery intent on seeing ghosts, but it was the spirit of the cemetery itself, I think, that I encountered… and it didn't like my presence.

During the 1870s, a shot of whiskey cost one bit (12.5 cents).

IV

D STREET RESIDENCE

This true location shall remain anonymous.

Mines plunged to depths of 3,000 feet, and miners suffered in temperatures of over 120°.

THE HAUNTINGS

"Imagine running a hot bath, feeling the water coming out of the tap as hot. When the tub is full, sticking hand in tub and it's hot. Then getting in and the water is cold as *ice*. I mean painfully cold, like thirty-two degrees."

***

"And you won't sleep there anymore, either?"

My brother shook his head. "No way, never again."

"But what happened? Did you see something, hear something?"

"I don't know how to describe it," my sister added. "I just really felt that something there didn't want me anywhere near it. I won't go in there."

"And you?" I pressed my brother. "Will you at least go in there?"

"Well, I wouldn't want to. No, not at night, that's for sure."

"Well," I resolved aloud, "You know Mom and Dad are going to put me in there, since no one else will. No big deal. I'll sleep there."

My sister shook her head. "Good for you. But I wouldn't."

My brother nodded in agreement.

I looked up at the ceiling, and tried to relax. I moved my shoulders about and shifted uncomfortably. The room was very small, with barely enough room to fit the bed. It was very nondescript, and dark. The walls were a boring color. The left wall, where the bed was, was an exception in that it had patterned wallpaper. The floor was wooden and bowed from years of foot traffic. The entire room felt even smaller than its actual humble size. The ceiling finally became too boring for me, and I stared down past my toes at the huge, ancient radiator beneath the window. It was not on, and the room was actually very, very cold. I couldn't see much outside the window, as there was little light outside.

A shifting of the covers exposed one of my shoulders. The cold oozed over it. I shivered and wormed my way deeper into the blankets. Despite my efforts, I found myself struggling to stay beneath the sheets. I realized, suddenly, the covers were being pulled down and to the side. I frowned. My littler brother, I figured, must be under the bed playing a trick on me.

I quickly leapt over the edge of the bed and peeked into the darkness beneath. It was empty. The darkness was nearly complete under there, but I could just barely tell it was vacant. I guess it had been my imagination.

I climbed back into bed, and realized it was too warm for the blankets, after all. The air felt clammy and damp. I looked at the window, expecting to see some clue to the sudden change in temperature, though I don't know why. It was late spring, and the temperatures outside were still cold in the nights. Even as I pondered the situation, the temperature rose so much that sweat started breaking from my forehead. My lower back was getting damp from perspiration, too.

Now the air was really hot, and I could feel the dampness in the air thicken. The air filled with steam, and I could see it roiling as if pushed by an unfelt breeze.

It was so dark, but the observations seemed pretty distinct. I began sweating freely, and I was intensely uncomfortable. I got out of bed and hurriedly went over to the door. I flicked on the light switch, and was greeted with a room filled with a solid cloud of white steam. The air was now thick with moisture: I could just barely see the window in the far wall. The radiator below it was shooting out steam like there was no tomorrow. The very air became so hot it actually hurt my skin. I blinked away sweat from my eyes.

The door, I discovered, was locked!

I struggled against the handle, and fought to quell the panic rising in my throat. My heart was suddenly pounding, and I felt, if possible, even hotter. I screamed, and began slamming my fists against the door. I yelled Mom's name over and over again. I have no idea how long I was in that state, slamming into the door and screaming. It felt like forever.

Finally the door opened. My slamming into the door almost forced it shut as Dad pushed it open.

"What? What's going on here?" he asked curtly. His eyes bored into me with annoyance.

I forced my breathing to slow down to answer him, as if everything wasn't obvious. When I turned about to gesture to the room, however, I discovered it was in fact *not* obvious. The temperature was instantly back to normal, and the steam was gone.

I stammered to explain, but he was not a man who had much patience for nonsense. "It was super hot in here, and there was a fog in here!"

He did not immediately answer. It took him a moment to respond doubtfully. "Hot in here? It seems pretty chilly to me. And what's this about fog?"

"Steam!" I cried, "It was shooting out of the radiator!"
He gave me a sour look. "The radiators are all offline.
There was no steam coming from it, or any other radiator
in the house."

Then he noticed the walls were dripping with
moisture.

***

I remember it clearly. I was lying in bed, trying to
fall asleep, and a voice just started talking to me. It came
from the thin air, near the foot of the bed. I couldn't make
out the words clearly, and they had an unusual melodic
quality to them, like some other languages have a
tendency to sound. The voice was so quiet, but was
obviously directed towards me.

I blinked in surprise, and stared at the empty air.
Suddenly the foot of the bed began to bounce, as if some
person were intentionally jumping on it. I couldn't believe
it… I was in shock! After a minute or two, however, the
bed stopped its violence.

I sat up in bed, panting heavily. My eyes were wide
with the expectation that it would start again at any
moment. Time clicked away. All was silent.

Eventually… and I'm sure it took hours… I managed
to fall asleep. I vaguely recall as I surrendered to sleep,
feeling a tugging at the foot of the bed.

When I awoke the next morning, my bed had been
turned ninety degrees and barely fit in the room in that
direction! My brother's bed, empty because he was

sleeping at a friend's house, was still straight. However, it was shoved against a different wall... and blocked the door.

***

The screams came at around 3:00 AM.

The shriek was from Mom. I ran out of my bedroom at the same time as my brother, whose room was next to mine. The cries came from the far end of the long hallway. A door was there, usually locked, which opened to a stairwell. From the darkness in the bottom of the stairs came the wailing.

My brother and I ran down to the end of the hall. The only light in the hall was from all the open bedroom doors. It was pretty dark in the stairwell. As I neared the top of the stairs, someone finally switched on a light in the hallway. From behind my shoulders came the light to paint my shadow on the walls... next to the blood.

The stairs were extra long. These were the back stairs, which went from the back yard outside all the way to here, the second floor. They were enclosed on both ends with doors, which were *always* locked. That night, for some reason, both doors were wide open, and there were trails of blood leading all the way from one to the other. Mom was at the base of the stairs, cradling Dad in her arms and crying. He was a bloody mess, and was shaking.

"What happened?" cried my brother.

Mom looked up. There were tears in her eyes. "Your father fell down the stairs."

"I didn't fall!" he exclaimed painfully. His face cringed in agony, and I saw his hand was broken and his fingers were all jutting into different angles. His face was streamed with blood, which emanated from his left ear. It had almost been ripped off from his violent tumble down the long, wooden stairs. "I was *pushed!*"

There were frowns all around at these words. My brother looked at me, and I just stared back. He absent-mindedly gripped his pajamas tightly. When I looked back down the long stairs to the scene, Dad met my eye. A look of fear, mixed with anger and, of course, pain, filled his features.

"You stay away from me!" he shrieked. "Don't you come near me again!"

I didn't know what to say. What was he talking about?

"Honey, what are you saying?" Mom asked him sternly.

"Him!" he brusquely replied. "He is going to the academy tomorrow!"

"But he has bronchitis! What are you saying? He didn't push you!!"

"Oh yeah?" he retorted angrily. "Well, it sure looked like him!"

"What?" I interjected. "What are you talking about?"

"Yeah," my brother added, "I saw him come out of his room at the same time as me."

"Honey," Mom asked Dad gently, "What were you doing all the way at the end of the hall? And why did you unlock the doors?"

Her question was very prudent. The only key to the door at the top of the stairs was in the kitchen downstairs. That applied to the door at the base of the stairs, too. Why would he have unlocked the door at the top *and* the bottom? The chill night air blew up the steps and into the hallway where my brother and I stood in our pajamas.

"I was going to the bathroom," Dad grunted. "I don't know how I got down here. I don't know why the doors were open, or who opened them. But I am not letting him get away with this!"

The events of the evening flashed through my mind. I had argued with my father earlier, though it was not one of our usual arguments. "I should have sent you away years ago," he had said, "If you weren't so damn sickly and weak, I would have sent you to a military school. I still might!"

"You don't understand me at all, do you?" I had replied.

Dad had been more than angry. His face had gone red with rage. We had argued for years, but this argument had held a sense of finality. For some reason, which I can't explain at all, I had been terribly calm. Usually I would shout right back at him. But that evening, the argument was different. I felt a sense of maturity in myself growing. Admittedly, I had been feeling really weak lately. I had been fighting some illness for two weeks now. I think it was bronchitis. Mom was scared it would turn to pneumonia.

"I'm tired of arguing with you," I had said. "You don't listen to me, and I won't ever be the way you want me to be. This will be our last argument."

Dad had been taken aback at my words. I don't think it dissolved any of his anger towards me, but I think, somewhere inside, he respected my words. He had shaken his head in resignation and, I imagine, disgust. We were simply too unlike each other, too different to see eye to eye.

We had parted on that note, and both stormed off to

our separate rooms.

And now he was accusing me of trying to kill him.

So I was sent to the academy. It was about a year later when I returned. The house was also part business, and some people came in one night when I was working with Mom. It was a couple that were in their later years in life. We got to talking, and they surprised me with a strange comment.

"You know, my best friend used to work here," said the woman. She was dressed in a thick winter coat and hat, for it was still early spring and quite cold. "He looked just like you. This was thirty years ago, of course, but he could have been your twin. He was the same size, too, but he had blond hair."

We began talking about the building and its history, and enjoyed ourselves. She returned a few days later with an old photograph of her and her friend from so long ago. She pulled the tattered, thick-papered photograph from her massive purse. They were both in their teens, and posing before an old car.

"Wow," I breathed. The young man in the photo reminded me sharply of what I see in the mirror every morning. "Whatever happened to him?"

She took back the photograph. "He died," she replied with surprising indifference. "It was a long, long time ago. He had pneumonia when he was about your age, and died in this house. He lived here, too, you see. An amazing coincidence."

An amazing coincidence, indeed. It was several days later, when I was about to meet my father for the first time since I had left, that I got to thinking a bit harder about the chance encounter with this older woman. A year ago, my father had claimed I had pushed him down the stairs... yet I had been in my room. And it was never explained how *both* the stairway doors had become suddenly and simultaneously unlocked. I realized suddenly it could have been none other than this spirit.

He had died in this house of pneumonia, this young man, and he had struck my father when I was fighting a similar illness. Perhaps he felt sympathy for me, or some sort of connection. A chill rippled down my back. To think this spirit would inflict such violence on my behalf was not a pleasant thought. I never bothered talking to anyone else in the family about my encounter with the woman or the information she brought to light.

***

"You'd be alone and by yourself in the house, and you could hear a radio upstairs in one of the bedrooms, and it would play music from the 40s, like big band stuff. There were no radios upstairs. In fact, there were no radios *downstairs*, because Dad didn't want us to be *corrupted*."

***

We moved into the new house on a frigid, February afternoon. Coming from southern California, seeing snow on the ground was more than enough to worry me about our new home. As soon as the truck pulled up to the house, slowing in front of the tall garage, I gazed anxiously up at it. It was a large house... it had to be, because I had three brothers and four sisters! Even before the big moving truck came to a complete halt, my youngest sister had wrestled the door open and was running towards the great structure. I watched Lisa go with mixed emotions. Something felt wrong to me about this house already... and it wasn't the novelty of snow.

I lowered myself slowly from the lofty truck, and scrunched towards the house. It was in need of repair, that much was obvious. It was large and drab, with a sagging backside. It appeared fully sound, of course, but I was used to a much more modern home in California, and this place was obviously pretty old. A breeze blew by and cut right through my flesh to the bones beneath, which it proceeded to saw into. I shivered painfully, and hurried towards the house.

Inside, I was immediately surprised that the place was furnished. I had not expected all the cupboards in the kitchen to be filled with plateware and glassware. A pile of old lamps sat alone in the corner of the living room, next to a few large stuffed chairs and an old, dusty couch. I was informed the place had not really been cleared after the last tenants. Mom didn't know why... or wasn't telling.

The afternoon went by quickly, as we had plenty of boxes to move. The girls had the task of organizing all the remnants from the previous owners, categorizing and moving the items into a semblance of order. Us boys helped Dad and Uncle Frank move the boxes. Dad didn't move too many heavy items, because he was overweight and in poor shape. That was part of the reason for us moving here, in fact... he couldn't keep up with the fast pace of southern California any longer. Uncle Frank, though... he was tough. He was an ex-Marine... and still lived like he was in the Corps.

Darkness fell early on, and we set up a number of lights. The electricity was not working yet, though it was supposed to be on already. Dad left to go work that out, while the rest of us continued hauling boxes under the headlights of the truck and Mom's car. Inside the house there were a lot of candles, and the fireplace was roaring in the living room. That was a good thing, too, because there was no heat in the big house yet, either.

On several occasions, while setting down a box in the house, I would glance up and catch a peek of other kids running past the windows. More than once I hurried over to get a better look, hoping there was some cool kids as neighbors… but they always were nowhere to be found. Considering how hilly the area is, it would not be that hard to get out of sight. Still, we lived at the end of the street… a dead end into the garage.

Finally we stopped work and ate a dinner of pizza, served on boxes and crates. It was freezing outside, and the wind was howling pretty loudly. Every now and then a gust would come down the chimney and the fire would flare. You could hear the groan of the wind through the many steep streets of Virginia City, and there was the flapping of a loose wooden gate, or a can would roll down a hill, blown over by the wind. I wasn't sure if I liked it here. The house felt strange to me. Everyone else seemed oblivious. Maybe I was just homesick.

The night passed slowly. All of us kids slept in sleeping bags around the fire in the living room. Mom and Dad were upstairs in the big bedroom, which had a bed. Uncle Frank had returned to his house, which was also in town. I lay there and listened to the wind hammer the building. It would shudder from the blow, and I would occasionally wince at a particularly strong gust.

I drifted in and out of sleep. It was so cold... and the house continued to feel...wrong. I dreamt I woke up the next morning, and it was warm and sunny outside... just like home was. The sun streamed into the house, and the gentle breeze brought the smell of flowers in. Kids were playing outside, laughing and running around the house. There were three girls and three boys... they were all brothers and sisters, like us. I got up and shook off the sleeping bag. I called out to one, the tallest boy with blond hair and a red sweatshirt. He turned and looked at me with surprise. As if on cue, all six of them started running for the house. One came in every entrance: the tall boy in red through the sliding-glass door, another through the front door, another through the back door, another through the side kitchen door.

As soon as they actually entered the house, I suddenly felt icy cold. I shivered uncontrollably, and they all ran straight for me. Their faces contorted into horrible, screaming masks... and their noses melted away and their eyes got bigger and bigger as they neared me, until their faces all turned into skulls. I screamed.

I woke up violently, and shivered. Cold wracked my body, but I was sweating profusely, which the cold just used to pierce deeper into me. Nobody else had awakened, and I was alone in the large, dimly lit room. Orange figures danced on the walls and cavorted along the slumbering forms of my brothers and sisters. A painful, freezing wind blew across my sweaty forehead.

I gasped as I looked around the dark house. The sliding glass door was all the way open... as was the front, the back, and the side kitchen door. Snow blew in through the open portals, spinning as it entered the house. I didn't have to check: I knew Mom and Dad hadn't opened the doors.

I think it was those kids in my dream. Somehow, I *knew* it was.

A few months passed, and we were all getting used to the new house. It was much bigger than our place in southern California, so we were all pretty happy. Even though it was so much bigger, all four of us boys still slept in the same room together with bunk beds. At least we had a separate bathroom from the girls.

I was still getting bad vibes from the house... more so now than before, in fact. I discovered the house had remained empty for almost two years before we bought it, and was sold with all the stuff from the old owners. We were planning a garage sale to get rid of most of it. Summer was finally nearing, and we were all anxious to explore all the hills around town and follow the dirt trails on our bikes, but Mom had us helping tag old junk all day. There was so much of it. We tried to get our sisters to do all the garage sale stuff, but it didn't work.

I was lying in bed one night, and I felt the bad vibes again. It was not a constant thing... it came and went. Usually I would dream about the same group of kids I had that first night, when I had the nightmare about them charging into the house and their faces turning to skulls. I could only make out the face of the one boy, the tall one with blond hair and the red sweatshirt. None of the others could be made out clearly. Whenever I would dream about them, I would wake up feeling chilled and almost sick to my stomach.

The dreams were always the same in this one regard: I would always be looking out the window at them. They would be doing different things, but I was always inside, and they were always outside. It was never our bedroom window, here on the second floor, but the downstairs one.

We were all settling into bed. My youngest brother, who sleeps beneath me, came stumbling out of the bathroom. His pajamas were soaked from where he leaned against the wet counter, I noticed. The same thing happened to me all the time. He crawled into bed, and then we heard the sounds.

Children playing.

It was about nine PM, and we could hear kids playing outside. We all had learned there were no other kids that lived on our block, and certainly we hadn't heard anyone playing this late before. However, I had told my youngest brother Davy about my dreams. He leaned out of his bed and looked up at me.

"Ken!" he whispered. "Do you hear that?"

"Yeah!" I whispered back.

"What do you think it is? Do you think it's the kids in your dream?"

"I don't know. I hope not!"

"What kids?" asked William from across the room in a fierce whisper. "You dream about kids, too?"

"Yeah. There are three girls and three boys."

"Oh my God!" he cried, "Me, too!"

"You mean, you dream about them, too?" I asked.

"Yeah! A lot. They are always playing outside. I can only make out the features of one of them. He's as tall as me, I think, and has dark blond hair. He is wearing a sweatshirt that says White Sox."

"I can only make out one, too," I replied. "He is the tallest, and has blond hair and a red sweatshirt."

The sounds from outside continued.

"Do you hear that, too?" Davy asked William across the room. He nodded, yes.

"What about you, Danny?" William asked to my other brother, up above him.

"You've had the dream, too, right?"

Danny, the second youngest, rolled over to face the rest of us. His face was pale in the dim light coming from the hallway. "Only once."

"Did you see the same number of kids?" I asked in a strained whisper.

He nodded mutely. Silence fell between us then, though we could all hear the unmistakable sounds of kids playing outside. We all cast frightened glances towards the window. The shade was pulled down, and my eyes focused intensely upon the ring at the end of the string, on the bottom. Did I want to pull on that, and see what was out there? It hung there, motionless… waiting.

We all exchanged glances, and all knew what the other was thinking. We all wanted to know what was out there… was it the children from our dreams? Or something normal? But no one wanted to be the one to open the window.

"William," Davy whined, "You open it."

He shook his head. We all knew he was the brave one. "No way. You do it."

Davy fiercely shook his head. To further illustrate his point, he snuggled deeper into his covers. I realized it would be up to me.

"I'll do it," I said. "I'm the oldest."

I slunk out of my top bunk, and slid to the floor as quietly as I could. My pajamas caught on something and got yanked up awkwardly, and I had to tug them back down. The wooden floor was strangely cold to my bare feet. It was usually cool at night in Virginia City, but suddenly I was really, really cold. I shivered, and noticed I could see my breath. It couldn't have been just my imagination. I looked at the others, and they were all absent-mindedly pulling their blankets up. It was too dark for me to see if any of their breath was showing, too.

I slowly approached the window. I could picture the tallest boy clearly in my mind. They were all playing a word game, I realized. They didn't sound like they were running around or anything, but all together and playing that word game Madlibs, or something. They were laughing a lot.

I neared the window, and stretched out my hand slowly to the ring near the floor. I had almost touched it when suddenly we all heard a deafening screech, like a car locking its brakes at great speed, and a thunderous crash. It was all so sudden, so loud, and so clear that I dropped to the floor instinctively and covered my head. I heard Davy cry out behind me, and I think I heard Danny whimper a bit, too.

Silence. Cold, dead silence.

I slowly raised my head, and looked to everyone else. Their faces were all white in the dark room, and their eyes wide with fright. My heart was pounding in my chest, so scared was I by the sudden and violent sounds. I listened, but I couldn't hear the kids anymore. Regardless, it didn't seem to help me with my task at hand any. I still didn't want to open the window, but now I was even more curious.

Taking a deep breath, I gripped the ring and tugged the shade all the way down to the floor. I let it loose, and it flew upwards and slammed into the spring mechanism at the top with a loud snap. Even before I looked up, I heard all three of my brothers screaming their heads off behind me.

I looked up, and right in front of me, the window was filled with the figures of the six kids. The three boys were up higher than the girls, and they all had their faces pressed against the window. Their faces were bloody ruins, and they slowly rubbed them harder into the glass, leaving streaks of smeared blood. I couldn't make out the faces of any of them, just bloody, mangled wrecks... except the tallest blond boy. His features were clearly visible to me. His nose was welling thick, deep red blood, which was gushing out and streaming all over the window.

I screamed louder than I think I ever had before in my life!

Mom and Dad both came running down the hall... I could feel their heavy footsteps as the floor shook. I turned away from the hideous image, and saw light stream into the room from the hall. Mom had turned on the light, and Dad's big frame filled the doorway. All my brothers were whimpering and hiding under their sheets. When Dad asked me what happened, I couldn't answer. I just pointed to the window... but it was empty.

It had only been two weeks since the night when we all saw the bloody faces of the kids in the window. We were not all dreaming the same thing at the same time, obviously, though Mom and Dad were having a hard time thinking otherwise.

I remember we were all in the living room, watching the Sunday night movie on TV. I heard the sounds in the distance I dreaded to hear: kids playing. It was the word game we had all heard together. I had been hearing this over and over lately. I knew what was coming. I sat there and tried not to listen. A commercial came on, and I fought to pay attention to it, instead.

Children playing... then the sound of a car screeching its brakes from a hundred miles an hour... then WHAM! The car crash seemed so close... so loud! I twitched at the impact, and I noticed William cringed, too. To my surprise, my sister Lisa nearly jumped at the very same moment. Mom and Dad shared a look after noting everyone reacting at the same time.

This very same phenomenon reoccurred every three hours after dark like clockwork. It never stopped, all night. During the day all was quiet, though. Yet only us kids seemed to hear it.

"What just happened?" Mom suddenly asked.

We all looked over at her on the couch next to Dad. She seemed concerned, and obviously was not party to what was going on. "It's the car crash, Mommy," Lisa said. I did not know Lisa heard it, too. I thought it was just us boys.

"The one you told me about, sweetie?"

Lisa nodded mutely.

Mom frowned, and looked to Dad. He shrugged.

"I didn't hear anything," he said.

"Well, neither did I, but obviously the kids did."

"Well, what do you want me to do about it?" he asked, irritated.

"I don't know."

"It's the garage," I volunteered. "There's the sound of a car driving like a hundred miles and hour, and then it slams on its brakes. It screeches awfully loud, and then it sounds like it slams into the garage."

"Yeah," Lisa agreed. "It hits the garage... but there's nothing there. We can hear it all night. We look for a car driving down the street and into the garage, but there's nothing."

Dad sighed. "Well, I don't know what I can do. If nothing is there, then nothing is there."

"I'm going to ask Frank to spend the night in the room above the garage tomorrow," Mom asserted. Dad's shoulders drooped.

"You don't need to bother Frank about this."

"Yes, I do. The kids are all obviously hearing something, and they all feel safe when Frank is around."

Dad sighed again.

"All right. Call him. It might be a good idea, after all."

We continued watching the movie, but all of us kids had our minds on Uncle Frank. If anyone could stand up to the horrible sounds, it was him.

The next evening, Uncle Frank came over. He had a sleeping bag with him, and threw it into the room above the garage. We all clustered around him as the sun lowered in the west. He knew what was expected of him, and he gave a grand show of confidence.

"You know, kids," he said, "I was a Marine for twenty years. I served in Korea, and I was a professional boxer, to boot. Nothing scares me. I'll find out what's going on for my favorite kids."

An hour or two later I was lying in bed, but wide-awake. Mom had a really hard time putting all of us kids to bed that night. None of us knew what was going to happen… but we felt *something* would. Uncle Frank seemed very unconcerned, and we could hear him downstairs in the kitchen laughing with Mom and Dad. Time passed, and eventually we heard Mom and Dad coming upstairs to bed, and Uncle Frank entering the room above the garage.

Time passed so slowly. We all tried to sleep, but we couldn't. We knew it wouldn't be long before we heard the sounds. The question was, would Uncle Frank?

Then I heard it. The kids... playing Madlibs. Laughter. I cringed, and gripped my pillow tightly. Then came the ghastly screeching, and the final, painful slamming of metal on metal. I shook with the impact. The sounds, deafening and horrible, faded away... but we immediately heard Uncle Frank. He was shouting.

"Anne! Anne!" Mom answered him as she ran from her bedroom. Uncle Frank burst loudly into the house and stormed up the stairs. We could hear their conversation clearly. He was panting.

"Anne, get the kids out of this house! Now!"

"What do you mean? What did you see?"

"Listen to me! You can all spend the night at my house. Get the kids' things and let's go!"

"Frank, what's wrong?"

"Anne, do you remember what I said happened to the previous owners of this house?"

"Why, yes, but..."

"I just saw it all! Just like it happened! The whole carload of them coming back from the Grand Canyon. The kids were playing a game, and the father fell asleep behind the wheel. Anne, I saw it all! I heard it outside, and ran down to see it. I saw the semi coming from over my shoulder and slam right into the car... right here in the garage! It was a bloody mess, Anne, and I don't want the kids to ever have to see it! All of them were dead and mangled by the side of the road... but inside the garage. It was clear as day!"

***

Things would move around in the house. We would never see it, but in the mornings things would be rearranged. Little things, mostly, not like furniture or anything. We all knew somebody was there... this old lady. We all saw her from time to time out of the corner of our eyes, out in the garden or wherever.

I was tasked one day to investigate the attic, you know, the crawlspace above the ceiling. We had been hearing some things from up there for a while, and Mom wanted me to check it out. Honestly, my brothers and I assumed it was the old lady, but Mom never wanted us to talk about such things. She either didn't believe in any of it, or didn't want to encourage us to believing it. Whatever, I know what I had seen time and time again.

So I got a stepladder from the garage, and wrestled it upstairs. The trap door in the ceiling... the only access to the crawlspace... was near the stairs. So I set the ladder at the top of the stairs... right up to the edge. It was kind of nerve-wracking climbing the stepladder at the brink of those steep, old stairs. But it was an old building, and you have to deal with things like that. My brother was there, too, and he stood at the top of the stairs, just in case the ladder somehow moved.

I made my way up to the top step, and hunched down below the trap door. It was a flat off-white color. I assumed it just pushed upwards, so I pushed up on it. There was some resistance. I applied more force, but did not get any better results. Frowning, I pressed my back against it, with my arms bracing along the ceiling for balance. The trap door shifted quickly with this superior strength, but it began immediately to wobble from poor balance. Obviously some weight was resting on it, and shifting about.

I reached up to balance it as it rocked, and my heart skipped when a long, blue and gray bird wing stuck down in my face. I nearly freaked from the surprise of the feathers jutting in my face as I pushed the door to the side. A dead pigeon tumbled down right in front of my face and nearly struck my brother below. I heard him grunt with disgust at the dead, twisted pigeon at his feet.

Meanwhile, I was still struggling with the trap door. It was not moving to the side easily: something was blocking it. I could tell right away there was another dead pigeon beginning to fall through the opening. I grimaced, but pushed the trapdoor to the side. Finally I shoved it strongly enough to displace whatever was in the way. The blackness above was deep, but along the edge there was enough light to reveal several dead birds. My grimace deepened.

I pulled my flashlight from my back pocket, and peered into the blackness above. I remained hunched below the opening, because I didn't want to just thrust my head in there with so many dead birds all around. I couldn't see much from this angle, however, and was forced to raise myself up.

Inside the crawlspace were not just a few more dead pigeons… but piles and piles of dead birds. It was a mass grave with dozens upon dozens of dead birds. There was probably over a hundred dead pigeons in the crawlspace there, all mangled and embracing each other with stiff wings. The smell was musty and foul… but not really strong. My heart jumped into my mouth. It totally freaked me out, and I nearly fell from the ladder.

I have no idea how all those birds came to be in that space, but they were piled up solidly. It was the creepiest thing I have ever seen.

Once we found all those dead birds... we never heard anything from the attic again. And, further, we never saw the old lady again, either.

***

"After my grandfather died... I remember I told my grandmother, 'He's not dead.'

"She said, 'Yes he is.'

"'He's not dead. Every night he opens the kitchen door, he comes in and makes a cup of coffee.'

"And she says, 'No, he doesn't. He's *dead*.'

"He had been dead maybe three weeks. My grandmother was sitting in the living room, and all of a sudden I came down the hallway and into the kitchen and I was like, 'You're here. Don't go anywhere! Wait here!'

"I went back, ran into the living room and said, 'You don't believe me? Go in the kitchen, he's in there right now. Come and talk to him.'

"She came into the kitchen and she saw him. She dropped her cup of coffee and started yelling at him to 'get out and never come back.'

"'That's my grandfather! Don't tell him to get out!'

"She said, 'Don't encourage him. He needs to know it's over.'

"I said, 'But maybe he wants...'

"She interrupted me, 'He's *dead*. End of story.'

"He never came after that again."

THE HISTORY

The area of D Street just south of the main business district was once the main entertainment district of Virginia City. It was lined with gambling halls, dance halls, saloons... and bordellos. This was the red-light district. The Old West frontier was renowned for its brothels... and Virginia City, the richest of all, was no different.

"A census conducted in August, 1860, showed 2,390 men in Virginia City and only 118 women, or a ratio of more than twenty to one. While never officially legalized by ordinance or statute, prostitution was nonetheless regulated to an extent. There were three main districts where this activity was allowed – the main red-light district on North D Street, the rude bordellos of Chinatown, which housed only Oriental women, and the infamous 'Barbary Coast' area of South C Street. The only licensing required, however, was for those establishments which sold beer or liquor." [1]

SOILED DOVES (PROSTITUTION ON THE COMSTOCK)

Prostitution was a noteworthy, if not entirely accepted, facet of Comstock life. Law enforcement had many legal euphemisms for it, such as 'running a disorderly house' and 'violating city ordinance'. Ironically, it was not only a legal, but also a much-loved profession. For example, the many admirers of local favorite Julia Bulette granted her an honorary position on the Virginia City Fire Company.

"Mining in the 19th century generally attracted a large number of single men. Predictably, prostitutes recognized the opportunity this represented. There is evidence that these women did not flock immediately to the Comstock, apparently fearing that it would fail, like so many other booms had. By the early 1860s, they established a red-light district on D Street, just below the main commercial corridor of Virginia City." (2)

In the beginning, there was such a lack of the female gender on the Comstock that any woman was accorded considerable honor. It was years before there were enough proper wives and mothers in the area to drive these 'working women' into the red-light district.

The profession of prostitution has generated far more intrigue than its relatively low numbers of participants would warrant. In 1870 there were at least 161 prostitutes in Storey County, but they never represented a significant part of the population. Still, these soiled doves exerted enormous influence. The successful madams were noteworthy businesswomen, and many entered into the profession only after recognizing how lucrative it could be, and for no other reason. (3)

It was not uncommon for a 'fallen angel' to hold a considerable amount of class, defying a frequent misconception of pitiful, victimized young women. Many of the madams were well dressed and highly successful, and surrounded themselves with the finer things in life, such as adorning their homes with fresh flowers (rushed from the west coast by Wells, Fargo and Company express). For many, service required knowledge of fine wines and French cuisine. Prices were raised accordingly, with payments of $1,000 a night not uncommon for perceived quality... during an age when a dollar bought a hearty meal.

However, not all prostitution was so successful. There were just as many women who eked out a meager existence in deplorable conditions. Brothels may have been numerous, but single-room, shack-like cribs were equally prevalent. Chinese prostitutes were not even allowed in the red-light district, but forced to remain in Chinatown, several blocks downhill. Destitution and alcoholism were frequent, while abuse, disease and crude abortions were not so obvious.

The whore with a golden heart was less than a reality, but certainly was more than a myth. Julia Bulette nursed hundreds of miners in her house-turned-hospital when they became ill from drinking polluted water. During the Civil War she raised much money for the charitable Sanitary Commission. Notorious madam Jessie Lester donated much of her estate to the Daughters of Charity, and was even buried in the sacred ground of the Catholic Cemetery.

WORKS CITED

1. Virginia City and the Silver Region of the Comstock Lode, p.74
2. The Roar and the Silence, p.176-177
3. The Old West: The Miners, pp.153, 157

V

THE OLD FUNERAL PARLOR

John Mackay ordered from Tiffany's an elaborate service set containing 14,718 ounces of silver. The 1,214- piece order, the latest in his wife's indulgences, required 200 silversmiths and 2 years to complete.

This location comprises the corner of an authentic Comstock-era block of structures. Behind it an outdoor deck offers fantastic one hundred-mile views over Six Mile Canyon and the dramatic deserts beyond. This site is unique to this volume in that it focuses on the building's original purpose and not the current business.

THE HAUNTINGS

I don't necessarily believe in ghosts. I do not disbelieve, either... especially after what happened to me upstairs one night. My wife frequently comments upon feelings of unease in the room upstairs. That, probably more than any other reason, is why it has become my workshop. I was working late one night on a project for a friend... upstairs, of course. I have no idea what time it was, because I was thoroughly engaged with what I was doing.

The area is not open to the public or anything, and is full of my junk. It is obvious from the look of the place it is a workshop. It is filled with all sorts of tools and miscellaneous stuff. Hanging on the wall beside the workbench is a rack filled with hand-tools, mostly woodworking equipment, and on the back wall hangs a large canoe. All of the objects in the room are a washed-out light brown... from all the sawdust that floats around and never gets out a window. The windows to C Street open, but they let in too much gusty wind at night, so I leave them closed most of the time.

It was dark outside, and it was cold as can be. When I had first come up, my breath was a very visible, frosty companion. I'm not sure how much time passed before I got into my work, and took off my winter coat. It was still cold in the poorly insulated upstairs, but my job is very physical. I hurled the coat onto the canoe hanging behind me, and crossed over to the router.

I began working, and time seemed to just disappear. It was getting pretty late... I know that much... but when I am using the router, I never pay attention to what's going on around me. I was hunched over the large machine, and squinting into a billowing cloud of sawdust. I strained to hold my hands steady against the power of the machine; the muscles in my arm jumped and jerked, but my hands were steady. A drop of perspiration silently fell onto the wood, and quickly gripped as much sawdust as it could.

Suddenly I was crushed in a painfully tight grasp from behind. Instantly my hands flew away from the router for safety's sake, and I reared back into the strange, smothering embrace. The back of my neck and shoulders were tightly squeezed, and I could feel something sliding around my shoulders to fully encircle my neck. A flare of shock jolted through me. The air had a strange feeling of something being horribly, terribly wrong. I forcefully ripped at the assailant, which instantly gave way. It all began and ended in a flash.

Tightly gripping my assailant, I looked down at it. In my hand I held my heavy winter coat. I just stared at it in mute incredulity, my heart pounding from the shock and adrenaline. The feeling of total wrongness fled as quickly as the attack had come. The sawdust whirled irately around me, and I could feel it plaster onto my sweaty forehead.

Slowly I turned and regarded the canoe, where I had hung my coat. It was *ten feet* behind me. Even if my coat could have fallen off and somehow made its way to me, there is no way it could have wrapped itself around me so tightly. No way! I regarded the room about me, but all seemed normal. In fact, it all seemed painfully normal. I kept expecting things to be different, but they were not. All I could hear was the noisy motor of the router, and watch the settling dust. Little eddies of sawdust spun about my feet, but that was it.

I shrugged off the encounter and stomped over to

the canoe. I regarded it skeptically, but it just hung upon the wall, oblivious to my suspicion. Finally, with a last look at it, I slung my heavy coat over its edge once more. In hindsight, when I felt such strong sensations of abnormality, I think it was a feeling of mischief more than any actual malevolence. Regardless, I returned to work, and did not encounter it again.

***

This building used to be a funeral parlor. Indeed, it was actually a very popular one, if popular is the right word. Successful, I guess. Anyway, downstairs is where they would dress up the deceased before they were buried. During winter, it was not uncommon for them to be kept there for a while. I guess it's no surprise many people claim a number of spirits reside there. Not everyone believes in ghosts, I realize, but I certainly do.

We were getting ready for a wedding one day last summer. The store was not yet set up, and there was a great amount of wide, empty space. That was why we chose to get everyone ready here, because it was a big wedding. Anyway, it was the ladies only that day, and we were having a great time with the wedding dresses and all the usual pre-wedding things. At the time there were eight of us in the room, and we were all having fun. There was no stress for this wedding, I can assure you.

We started taking pictures of everyone, just for ourselves. These weren't the usual posed wedding photos or anything, just everyone with a camera trying to get a snapshot of the good times. The sun was streaming in from the windows overlooking the canyon; so many of the shots weren't working unless they were against the north wall. All the walls were bare and clean white, so against the north the photos turned out really well.

The subject of the building came up, which is not surprising, as the store was just being started and everyone wanted to know about my latest project. I told them the place used to be a funeral parlor, and there were supposedly a lot of ghosts in the basement. They all thought that was quite a story, so I drug the whole lot of them downstairs to see. There wasn't anything to see, of course, but you know how it is. We joked around downstairs for a bit, but just as we started back upstairs, I stopped and said to the room in general, "Hey, we are taking a group photo upstairs. Anyone who wants to be in it, come on up!"

The girls all laughed at that, and I did, too. But there was certainly no laughter when I got my photos back. We were all posed against the north wall, with the camera set to automatically take the photo. We were all in the same dresses as bridesmaids, except the bride herself, of course. What takes my breath away, even when I think of it now, is there were not eight of us in the photo.

There were ten.

Two men were in the photo, with huge, thick mustaches and wearing clothing from the 1800s. Both were on a knee before us, posing for the camera.

***

"When I was visiting my friend Pat, I was waiting for her in the main room. She was upstairs, I think. I was just wandering around, and then I felt a chill sink into my bones. The hair on the back of my neck stood up, and started prickling me as my scalp tightened.

"I felt a hand slide into my right front pocket. There was no one else there… just me. I freaked, and hurried towards the door, but the experience stopped as I neared it. There was no mistaking it, though. Someone… or some*thing*… put its hand in my pocket."

Both Virginia City and Lake Tahoe have the same elevation (roughly 6,200 feet).

THE HISTORY

A year after the great Fire of 1875, this building was reconstructed by C. Ciandoni. For over half a century it was a funeral parlor, begun by the Kitzmeyer family of Funeral Directors.

Rumor has it that when Virginia City's famed and beloved prostitute Julia Bulette was murdered, Mr. Kitzmeyer personally handled all the preparations for her funeral. He was so taken by her in life that his generous donations of time and money provided for a very fine funeral. Further wild speculation claims he was so smitten with her that she may have never actually left the basement. Julia's funeral was during the frigid winter months, when no graves could be dug. It is a matter of fact that her profession led to her having two burials in separate locations. Two burials... yet not a single body.

There is still evidence of this structure's original occupational design. Along the north wall, nearly hidden among the old bricks, is the outline of an archway. Such alcoves (beneath the street above) may have held bodies in waiting for the spring thaw. All were bricked up long ago. The concrete floor of the basement is modern, and a hole drilled entirely through it teases speculation of whether bodies... perhaps even Julia herself... still lie beneath.

Despite such celebrated burials as above, the majority of the funeral parlor's business inevitably came from the premature death of the thousands of miners that toiled below ground every day.

DEATH IN THE MINES

The Comstock was not an easy place to live. The number of men who worked the mines can never be truly known, though it has been estimated at some 10,000. At least 300 of these men were killed in the mines, and 600 maimed or crippled. "There were periods when a man was killed every week, and another grievously injured every day." [1]

Miners were frequently stricken with occupational diseases such as pneumonia and rheumatism. In the mines men collapsed from heat exhaustion. Temperatures hovered between 120-130°. Eventually the temperatures in the mines rose 5° for every hundred feet of depth. Water heated to as much as 160° spurted out of drill holes. In one mine the daily allotment of ice went up to ninety-five pounds per worker. Wooden pick handles became so hot miners had to wear gloves. Working time was reduced to fifteen minutes out of each hour. Outside was little better, with the winters at the lofty elevation of 6,200 feet on the slopes of the snow-capped Mt. Davidson bitter indeed.

"Falls were the most common cause of death. At the end of their shifts, as they came up swiftly from the caldrons to the cool air, miners sometimes became faint and fell. Their bodies ricocheted down the shaft, being torn apart by repeated impact on the timbers, until a rain of fragments reached the bottom and fell into the sump, a pit full of hot water. Small grappling hooks were kept on hand to recover the pieces, which were rolled in canvas or put into wooden candleboxes to be taken above." [1]

In the underground levels of the mines, another common reason for falling was when miners thoughtlessly pushed cars into empty shafts. Apparently assuming that an elevator is waiting, an unwary man's car will drop suddenly into oblivion, and pull him with it. When cages are descending into these lower levels, sometimes men take a peek at a passing station. Their heads momentarily enter the horizontal shaft and are instantly crushed or pulled off entirely as the heavy iron cage continues downward.

"Other common causes of death were the premature explosion of blasting charges and the falling of timber, tools and other objects down the shafts. In 1880, in a mine called the New Yellow Jacket, a car loaded with steel drills was being hoisted to the surface. Near the top it caught on an obstruction - probably one of the drills struck a timber - and spilled its contents into the adjoining compartment of the shaft. The drills fell half a mile and struck eight men in a car on the 2,800 foot level, killing five instantly and injuring others." [1]

Massive engines are required to haul the iron cars laden with heavy ore up and down these shafts of thousands of feet. Equally impressive is the thick steel cable connecting the engines with the cars. Sometimes these wires will snap under the strain. Any men who happen to be in such a car will be protected by several safety measures, such as automatic brakes and protective roofs. However, the cable is liable to spring backwards and kill the engineer at his station at the head of the shaft.

"A heavy cable of steel wire, whipping back in this way, will cut a broad road through the whole length of the ceiling of a building, taking off large joists and beams as though they were so many bars of soap. Huge fly-wheels of many tons' weight occasionally burst asunder, tearing the sides and roof of the works to pieces, killing or wounding all who may be in the way of the flying fragments; boilers sometimes explode and leave hardly a vestige of the works in which they stood; men are caught in cog-wheels of the machinery; and, in short, there is no safety either above or below the ground." [2]

WORKS CITED

1. The Old West: The Miners, pp.73,76
2. The Big Bonanza, p.152

Virginia City is America's largest Historic Landmark.

VI

C STREET

The most direct route between the lode and Truckee Meadows was constructed by Davison M. Geiger, after whom Geiger Grade was named. The harrowing and steep curves, such as Robber's Roost and Dead Man's Point, provided ample opportunities for stage robbers.

Nevada State Highway 341 becomes C Street while running through Virginia City, and continues on towards Gold Hill and past Silver City. The C Street corridor was always the center of the financial district. Currently the stretch is illuminated nightly with old-fashioned gas lamps. Much of the original boardwalk remains as well.

THE HAUNTINGS

I live in an old Victorian house off the main district of C Street. This is a large, quiet place with several of the rooms rented to tenants. It was late evening after a scorching day during the summer, despite being 6,200 feet in elevation. The sun had only recently dived beneath the cherry skies and past the pink-shrouded Sierra. The faint sound of revelry drifted down the mountain from the bar crowds above.

Suddenly my door rocked from a pounding. The door shook on its hinges as the hammering continued, and I rose to answer it. The door opened to reveal my fellow tenant and friend Lisa, panting madly and completely unkempt. Her hair was in disarray, and she appeared to be in only a half-state of dress. Lisa was young, and had apparently been preparing to go out to some of the bars before something stopped her. Her wide eyes met mine.

"Anna!" she demanded, "Come quick! You've got to see this!"

Pulling me along, Lisa led me through the large, dark house to her room in the back. Moonlight from outside somehow penetrated into the home and lit our path through the dark hallway. Sharp glares lined the many picture frames of the Comstock days that adorned the entire house.

We entered the bedroom, which was filled with scattered miscellaneous clothing. The bed was covered with several dresses. Lisa did not acknowledge the state of the room, but immediately strode over to the massive window that looks out behind the house. She anxiously beckoned me to come over.

"What's going on?" I asked in a comparatively calm and average voice. Lisa immediately shushed me, and then motioned once again for me to approach the window. The frantic Lisa pulled back the richly embroidered curtain and gestured outside.

With a quiet voice, Lisa explained, "They have been doing this for over five minutes now. Quiet. They are still here."

I crossed the room, stepping over some hastily discarded clothing, and peered out the window. The street below was dark, but relatively well lit with the pale white moonlight from above. The gas lamps did not extend to this portion of C Street. Despite the lack of any rain, the road appeared saturated and damp in the moonlight, though it was merely a trick of the night. The other structures that line the street were all dark.

In the center of the road, however, was something very, very unusual. Four tall, slender columns of mist were there, dancing about. Each anomaly was about the height and shape of a person, though there was no definition to any of the presences. They all danced and moved about the road in unison, wavering and wiggling. Back and forth they dipped and spun… for all appearance dancing to the music that rolled up the mountainside from further down C Street.

I stared in shock, and we both continued to watch the strange, surreal cadence of the four figures. They were comprised of nothing more than a dark mist, revealed only relatively well against the damp-looking street.

Together we watched the figures prance for another ten minutes before they just vanished into the night. We looked at each other, but neither of us said another word. I just shrugged, and left Lisa to continue preparing for her own night of dancing.

***

I was walking to a bar one night to meet with some friends for a drink. The sun had already set, and it was a dark night. It was winter, and the sky was filled with dark, menacing clouds that obscured any moonlight that may have wanted to light the area. I was walking from my house, which meets up with C Street on the north end of town. Behind me I heard a strange noise, but could see nothing. I heard lots of jingling, like heavy chains.

I looked around, but couldn't see anything behind me. I cocked my head to the side to listen a bit better, and could make out a sort of squeaking sound with it. Frowning, I realized the sound emanated from C Street, but back north... close to where the Fire Department is, actually.

Suddenly I saw movement from out of nowhere... well, the darkness I suppose! The sound suddenly roared loudly, and I saw a black coach come thundering by, led by a team of four huge black horses. Atop each horse was fixed a series of tall black plumes bouncing gaily as they fairly flew by. The noise of their hooves pounding was nearly deafening! I heard them snort with the strain of running uphill, and their sides were all flecked with foam. Then the cage raced by, black but with neat trimmings in some color that I couldn't make out in the dark. I only barely caught a glimpse of the driver, dressed sharply in black livery.

The whole thing just thundered on past me and up C Street into town. I watched it for another few hundred feet... and it vanished!

The Hauntings

***

We were driving from Virginia City to Carson City. I was new to the area, and had not visited the capital yet, so my friend Bob and I decided to make an afternoon of it. Bob was driving, and I was just looking around at the remnants of the glory days of the past.

As we continued downhill, I found myself getting very sick to my stomach. At first I thought it was just the fast car going down the steep curves and losing elevation so quickly... but it got worse. Finally I began to feel seriously ill, and I told Bob to pull the car over. He was surprised, but obliged. The vehicle ground to a halt on the side of the road, and I just stared at the dirt beside the road. I felt ill, but I didn't really think I was going to be sick or anything. Bob, I think, was mildly annoyed.

"Are you sick?" he asked bluntly.

"No," I responded slowly, unsure. He obviously could tell I was unsure.

"Well, we are half way there. Do you want to just keep going, or do you want to turn back?"

"Well, I guess I'm all right now. Let's keep going."

"Good!" he proclaimed, and was instantly pulling the car back into the road. Bob was nothing if not enthusiastic. As we progressed downhill, however, I began to feel an overwhelming urge to stop the car. I fought it, but finally had to tell Bob to pull over again. He was a little hesitant, but of course he obliged. We were a few hundred feet before a large stone outcropping that lined the road closely on each side. When I saw it, I suddenly knew I must not, under any circumstances, go between those rocks. I said as much.

119

Bob looked at me with a puzzled frown. "Are you serious?"

I nodded hurriedly. "I don't know why, but I cannot go through those rocks. I'm sorry."

"That's called Devil's Gate," Bob informed me. "That used to be a toll station, and was used as a station during one of the wars with the Indians...the Paiutes, I think."

"Well, I'm not going near it."

Bob looked at me with exasperation. "Dude, it's the main highway... and the only way to Carson that won't take us thirty miles out of our way. It's not much further."

"Look, something is wrong for me up there. Something is very wrong. Something very bad happened there."

Bob was well aware of my tendency to feel certain things in some places, so he fortunately refrained from a sarcastic remark. "What, did some robbers shoot a stage driver, or what?"

"I just feel death waiting for me there."

Bob shrugged, and then grudgingly turned the car around.

I found out later that near that very spot one of the Grosh brothers, the original discoverers of silver on the Comstock, had died. He accidentally struck his foot with a pickaxe, and it got infected. His blood became poisoned and his leg ceased functioning. He was confined to a chair for the remainder of his days, unable to walk. And his brother, Allen, had both his legs amputated from being frozen in a blizzard in he Sierras.

These facts are quite relevant, considering a few years ago I had both my legs amputated.

The Hauntings

THE PHENOMENON OF THE LITTLE GIRL

While conducting interviews for the source material of this book, I encountered many people. Sooner or later, I knew, I would encounter the same stories... but I had not figured on blatantly conflicting stories. But after all, we are only human, and ten people who witness the same event will tell it in ten different ways. Likewise, stories have a tendency to change as they pass from mouth to mouth.

One specific example of this revolves around the ghost of a little girl. Numerous interviewers reported sightings of her, with claims of her playing with the toy trains in a gift shop to playing with dolls in personal homes. Many people seem to feel almost an ownership of their encounters with her. I suspect this is due to the dual facts that we are speaking of an innocent (which plays upon people's sense of passion), as well as the frequency of encounters with this girl in a wide variety of physical locations.

All those asked were unanimous in recounting her untimely death: an accident on C Street involving a cargo-laden stagecoach that ran her down and crushed her. Yet any other details about this restless spirit are open to conjecture. Some claim she was the daughter of a prostitute working in the Millionaire's Club in the Old Washoe building, while others vehemently claim no children were allowed in the building at all.

Regardless, she is the most common thread of any ghostly encounters in Virginia City I have encountered. The following are a few recollections of her nightly visitations.

***

"Oh, yeah, we've seen signs of the little girl in the upper floors [of the Old Washoe Club]. The doors are locked all the time, of course. In the dust we have seen the footprints of little shoes. Are they a little girl's rather than a little boy's, well I don't know. I can tell you that neither have been upstairs, though!"

***

I should have been tired, but I wasn't. It certainly was late enough… though admittedly I am usually the type that stays up late. I don't recall exactly what time it was, but it was past even our bedtime, that's for sure! Andy had just rolled over onto his side, and was trying to fall asleep as well. We were both facing the wall, snuggling comfortably, if not very relaxed at the moment.

We had only been in bed a few minutes… not even that, really. We had just stopped maneuvering into a comfortable position, when I felt the presence. Even though we were both facing the wall, I could tell that someone was outside the bedroom door.

I cranked my head over to take a look. Despite the awkwardness of the move, I found myself frozen upon the sight of her. Yes, *her*. A child, a little girl, was hovering right outside the doorway, looking in. It was dark in the hall behind her, but the bedroom had a window that let in enough light for me to see her dimly. Her hair was blond, I noted, and very long. It was total blackness behind her, and she stared in with a strange intensity. Her features were too obscured with shadow for me to make out any expression, but her big eyes were riveted to Andy.

The house was locked, I knew. It was a very small place, an old miner's quarters in fact, moved up to C Street from down near the mines in Six Mile Canyon. I could sense that she did not belong to the house so much as the area in general. And, to be honest, I had heard of her.

It was the ghost of the little girl that had been run down in front of the Mackey Mansion... trampled to death by a team of horses. There she was... floating in my hallway, looking at my husband. I was too stunned to even gasp.

Before my wide eyes, she floated into the room. I did not see her legs move at all. She coasted through a beam of lamplight that pierced the room from the window, and for a second glowed brilliant white. She did not move a muscle... her arms were at her side and she leaned forward as she slid smoothly through the air. Her approach did not stop until she had crossed the entire room and was right beside Andy, who was snuggled behind me. She was merely two feet from him, looking down at his prone figure. Her large eyes looked black in this light.

I nudged him, but he didn't move. I didn't want to speak, or ruin the silence of the moment. Silence seemed more appropriate, somehow. But how could he be asleep already? We had just settled in mere moments ago. I couldn't see his face, which was nuzzled behind me, but his breathing was slow and even. My nudging should have been plenty to wake him, though. It's what I always do to wake him: Andy's a very light sleeper.

The little girl, still looking down at Andy, suddenly floated straight up and over him. Now she was looking down at him with her whole body at a very unnatural angle... unnatural to someone standing... or to a *human*. Her figure appeared solid, and her blond hair fairly glowed with the beam of lamplight behind her. She had a silk bow in her hair, I noticed. She was wearing a blue satin dress with ivory lace, which matched her bow. She seemed very nice, and continued gazing down at Andy. I had several moments to view her at my leisure.

Then she slowly raised her head and looked me in the eye. We locked eyes for a moment, and she smiled pleasantly. Her eyes were blue.

Then she vanished.

The next day I was in the Old Washoe Club, having a draught beer and talking to my friend, Sharon. Sharon was the owner of the Club then, and had seen many a ghost in her time there. I felt the need to speak with someone about it that would understand. Andy did not recall a thing. I can only surmise that he was simply not meant to experience the visitation.

"So," I was saying to Sharon, "She just floated up to Andy, and then over him. She said nothing, and stared at him with some sort of intensity."

"Tammy, did you see what she was wearing?"

"Yeah," I responded, thinking back. "She wore a blue dress."

Sharon nodded. "Yep, with white lace and a matching bow in her hair?"

I chuckled, and then nodded. "Yeah." I should have known that Sharon would know the details of this little girl.

"Yeah, she is in the Club all the time. She wanders the whole city, actually."

"So I've heard. She was really nice, though, if odd."

"Yeah, I heard that she was moving some toy trains down the street, at the train shop."

"Obviously," I replied. "Well, it's the first time I've seen her."

Sharon looked at me funny. "Probably not the last."

***

"During one of the ghost walk tours, you know, around Halloween, a guy was taking a photo of the spiral stairs. He was a tourist from out of town, so I don't know who he was. Anyway, he called back a few weeks later. He had developed the photographs, and in the mirror behind the spiral stairs was a young girl in a very old-style dress and wearing a bonnet. She was under ten years old, he said. She was standing with the rest of the group, just on the edge, and looking up at someone just outside the picture. I was just as surprised as he was, because there were no girls on that trip!

"There are a lot of sightings of the young girl. Some people claim that there were no children allowed in the Old Washoe Club, which makes sense. However, the building has been a lot of other things, too. People have seen the footprints of a young girl in the dust up on the upper floors, even though it is off limits."

***

"I was chatting with this new girlfriend of mine the other day, after our interview. You had reminded me of how much I love Virginia City, and how I want to move back there if I get the chance. Well, ironically enough, I found out that my friend also not only loves the town as much as me, but used to live there, too.

"'I love the people and the town itself,' I said to her, 'but I also love the spirits of the place.'

"'Me, too,' she said. I was shocked.

"'You've seen ghosts, too… and actually like them? Most people get freaked out by them.'

"'Yeah, I know,' she said, 'but I used to live in a little pink house up on the hill on C Street. You know that series of small, little homes across from…'

"'Across from the Mackey Mansion,' I finished. 'Yeah I know them. I used to live in the little pink one.'

"Her eyes got wide. 'Really? I lived there for years when I was a little girl!'

"'The pink one?'

"'Yeah!'

"'Wow!'

"'Anyway, I used to play with a ghost when I was growing up. A little girl and I would play… all night, sometimes. I miss that.'

"Now *my* eyes got really wide. 'What did she look like?'

"'She was my age… I was about eight or nine then. She wore a little blue dress with white lace, and she had long blond hair.'

"I just couldn't believe it. That is exactly who I saw, not five years ago, floating above Andy."

***

An important addendum directly relates to this phenomenon. Over the course of my interviews, a rumor repeatedly popped up of the discovery of ancient bones discovered in the courtyard behind the Old Washoe Club... the bones of a little girl. As the story goes, the electrical company was sent into the courtyard to complete some work when they unearthed the human remains.

I took pains to verify this fact with 3rd party confirmation, but all attempts failed. The electric company has no such records, nor do the owners of the building. The Storey County Sheriff likewise has no records of this event, nor the County Coroner. As far as I am concerned, this lays to rest any such rumors. True to form, however, such legends will undoubtedly persist.

Marie Mackay, wife of Comstock millionaire John Mackay, paid $15,440 for a portrait by a French artist that she hated so much she burned it.

THE HISTORY

C Street has always been a main thoroughfare and the foundation of the commercial district of Virginia City. Its length holds some distinctive features, such as the Territorial Enterprise, where Mark Twain developed his famous writing style, and the International Hotel, a six-story palace with the first elevator west of the Mississippi. C Street was a metaphor for the entire Comstock Lode in that it contained the finest and richest of appointments, as well as the darkest and most violent of elements.

THE BARBARY COAST

Virginia City has always had a dark element. In the 1860's, for example, when Virginia City had a population of 15,000 souls, there were one hundred gambling houses to only four churches. [1] The red-light district of D Street was considered a necessary evil to the upright citizens. It was avoided by those who wished to do so. An unavoidable blemish on their community, however, was the south side of C Street. This collection of prostitution cribs, brothels and tough saloons had a reputation for danger and mystery, and attracted only the hardiest and most adventurous of men. This was known as the Barbary Coast.

After The Great Fire of 1875 destroyed a majority of the red-light district, the Coast became even more of a haven for the city's prostitutes and toughs. Still, the actual numbers of brothels was likely far less than public opinion would offer. Intimations like those of Miriam Leslie, writing of her 1877 visit to Virginia City, for example, are more tantalizing than concrete. She pointed out, 'Every other house was a drinking or gambling saloon, and we passed a great many brilliantly lighted windows, where sat audacious looking women who freely chatted with passers-by or entertained guests within.' (2)

Brawls were more than common among 'Coasters'. One night a policeman ran into a saloon to see two men struggling upon the floor. The uppermost man rose from the prostrate and bleeding form of his antagonist as the policeman approached, and said, 'I'm a quiet man, a man who wouldn't harm a fly, but when I'm crowded too far, I will remonstrate!,' whereupon he spat out the nose of the man who was lying on the floor. (3)

Such sensational acts soon led to the second public execution of Virginia City. Owners of neighboring saloons, Irish immigrants Peter Larkin and Nellie Sayers, who had enjoyed a close relationship, broke ties when Nellie took up with Daniel Corcoran. Larkin then hired prostitute Susie Brown, but soon began quarreling with her as well. Susie sought protection from Nellie Sayers, who was now a vicious rival of Larkin. Early morning on August 4th, 1875, pistol fire sounded just moments after Corcoran chased a trespassing Larkin away from his house. Daniel Corcoran fell to the ground with a mortal wound to his abdomen. The police arrested Larkin, tried him, and convicted him of murder.

Following the opening of the Fourth Ward School, which forced children to walk through the Barbary Coast, intense efforts were made to clean up the area. Nellie Sayers herself was eventually arrested for running her brothel. She continued to run the business without a license, however. When it was discovered that she was offering her clientele a child prostitute, however, it was the last low that enabled the upright citizens to finally force the darker elements of the Barbary Coast back into the red-light district of D Street.

WORKS CITED

1. The Old West: The Gamblers, p.149
2. The Roar and the Silence, pp.178,185
3. The Big Bonanza, p.277

The Nevada state flag adopted in 1915 erroneously had 37 stars instead of 36.

VII

THE VISITOR'S BUREAU

Gold was a common ingredient in patent medicines sold for the relief of kidney complaints arising from excessive alcohol consumption.

The Visitor's Bureau is a glass-fronted store decorated in red, white, and blue. The pink second story is lined with tall windowed apartments. This structure is directly across from the large Comstock Monument, overlooking Six Mile Canyon. Inside the store all the walls are lined with shelves filled with old nostrums, outmoded medications, and drugs. Hundreds of antique bottles of medicines and boxes of pills wait in every corner. Also included are old measuring devices and laboratory equipment. Prescription and receipt books from over a century ago are also hidden inside.

The Hauntings

"My calculator would just kinda start calculating. It would be down on one end of the counter and I'd hear tick-tick-tick. It was always zeroes. I'm like, 'OK... [wondering what's going on].' It would just add and add and add. You couldn't stop it. It would either run out of paper, or run out of electricity."

***

The sun was bright outside, and its morning position let strong shafts pierce the shop through the front windows. The tops of the fifteen-foot windows were admittedly rather dirty, and the sunlight was mottled and brown as it streamed inward. The tainted beams were warm and the morning cheery. Despite this happiness, I was feeling dark and afraid. I did not really relish the thought of grabbing some merchandise from the hallway upstairs. Still, the store was going to be opening soon, and I needed to stock up on the impulse items for the counter. I was almost out of post cards, too, and had more up on the stairs and in the hall upstairs.

I opened the door somewhat hidden in the north wall and let my gaze first ascend the stairs. The steps were old and very steep: so steep in fact that going up on hands and knees was a serious consideration. They were only a few inches deep. These stairs were made a long, long time ago when there were obviously no building codes. They rose sharply, and near the top was an awkward landing, if it could be called that. The steps curved sharply to the left and out of view: they were only a few short, angled inches deep there, and a misstep could cause quite a nasty fall.

Sighing quietly, I followed the steps upwards. They were packed with as much merchandise as their narrow width would allow. Open boxes blocked the steps everywhere, with tissue and packing materials exposed. A few of the items I needed were on the stairs: I had placed as much there as possible to avoid having to go into the hallway upstairs. I brushed them all aside and steeled myself for the feelings that I knew I would encounter up in the hall.

I slowed as the steps arched painfully to the left. Far, far up above me was an open space topped with a skylight. The light cheerily poured into the hall and bounced about merrily. The white paint gave the hall a bright look... but not a clean one. It was thick with over a century of repeated applications, and ail the joints were brute and angles off.

Twenty feet above the crooked steps, in the side of the shaft, was a panel that blocked off the attic space. It was in such a strange, inaccessible spot. I was insatiably curious what was in there... but knew that *she* would never let me look without protest. This spot was very open and inviting, but the hallway extended in either direction into darkness, as the lighting was very sparse and ancient. It was in the tight, darkened hallway that *she* made her presence known... and her dislike of anyone entering her space.

I don't know for sure, but had been told that she was an old lady who had lived in the apartment above the shop.

She had spent years there, and had been extremely protective of her belongings. No one knew what she had that was so worthy of such desperate protection. Whatever it was, the spirit of the old woman made it clear to any entering the ancient, cramped hallway that they were not welcome. All I know is that I am extremely disliked by the spirit of this old woman.

I entered the hall and ran down the length into the darker areas. The rooms that lined the amazingly narrow width of the hall were all very small. These tiny, almost closet-sized rooms had at one time contained just enough space for a small cot. Now it was just enough room for some extra storage. I quickly dug through the boxes, worrying all the time how the old lady would express her displeasure this time. I felt exposed up here, crammed into the little rooms and bent awkwardly over boxes. My feet were barely pried into the small openings on the floor between boxes, and the angles were all just wrong to make me comfortable. If I had needed to run, I knew that it would take me too long to even turn around in here without twisting an ankle.

Still, I felt no enmity this time… no feelings of anger and fear. The sensations are sometimes subtle, sometimes strong. When they are strong, there may also be a feeling of… wrongness.

The old lady, named Helen supposedly, has never shown herself to me. Others claim to have seen a wispy, shadowy figure in this bizarre, unique hallway. Once I had gathered up all I needed to, I skipped back towards the beam of light that pierced the gloomy, ancient hallway. If that beacon had not always been there to light the way back down the crazy old steps, I don't think I would even have come up here at all. I never enter the hall at night unless I absolutely... *absolutely...* have to.

I sped down the stairs as quickly as I felt safe doing so. No encounter this time... fortunately.

***

"I was working one day in the Visitor's Bureau. I hadn't been there long. I'm not a regular employee or anything. I was just helping out my friend. Anyway, I was standing there behind the counter, when I heard this loud crack, and then the sound of marbles or something like that skittering across the floor. It was plain as day, the sound of all the stuff rolling away along the wooden floor. I found out later that this used to be a pharmacy back in the 1800s. There can be little doubt that what I heard was the sound of pills being spilled all over the floor. From the sound of all those pills rolling into corners, and having to pick them up... I would be mad enough to replay that day for eternity, too!"

***

"I don't know what the deal is with all the ghosts in Virginia City. I love this town, and have lived here all my life. I think that many people who encounter negative ghosts are just seeing reflections of themselves. I have lived here for decades... and never have I met an evil spirit. I have seen hundreds [of ghosts]. I love it. They just want some attention. They are mischievous, definitely, but they never mean any harm. They just want you to acknowledge them. I talk to them all the time, and they usually stop the pranks when you tell them to.

"They like to move things. There have been many mornings when I come in and things have been moved. In the middle of the floor, twenty feet from the shelf they are usually on, I will find things. I just put them back and jokingly chastise them."

Over 90% of the Lake Tahoe area was deforested by the late 1870s. Only one small section on the south shore retains original old-growth trees.

THE HISTORY

The original Pioneer was a pharmacy on the main floor with a front to C Street. This building is located right in the heart of the business district of old Virginia City's bonanza times. Mr. Paul Coryell operated the pharmacy continuously until 1949, when he closed the doors due to illness (at age eighty-two). In 1952 new owners reopened it. There was a boarding house upstairs with access from B Street. A communal bathroom was near the entrance on B, and the narrow hall was lined with small rooms for rent.

Doctors, dentists, midwives, and nurses made living in such a harsh environmental and social climate a bit more livable. In 1870 there were thirty-one doctors, nurses, and dentists on the Comstock, yet a mere five years later the number jumped to more than fifty. This meant that in 1875, Storey County had approximately 360 people for every health care provider.

Regardless of the number of professional healers in the area, folk remedies abounded. "Wood ashes or cob webs would stop bleeding; a bag of asafetida [brownish foul-smelling material obtained from the roots of the parsley family] worn around the neck could remedy a cold; a salve of kerosene and beef tallow softened chapped hands." Indeed, 'nurse' Mary McNair Mathews (she had no formal training), called upon sympathetic magic to protect her son after an accident cut off his finger. So it would not harm him in the future, she placed the digit in a jar of brandy. [1]

All types would make their appearances at Virginia City during its heyday, all hoping to cash in on the abundant wealth. Many would come selling absurd cure-alls made of petroleum, nostrums of all sorts, or bring electrical machines and apparatus for testing all manner of superfluous notions. These men were as apt to bring street-show acts, such as 'freaks from Africa', as they were to sell soap-root toothpowder. Comstock contemporary Dan DeQuille records the sales pitch of one such charlatan:

"Who is the next gentleman who wishes to try the battery? It makes the old man feel young, and the young man feel strong. Remember, gentlemen, that a quarter of a dollar pays the bill. Try the battery! Try the battery! Bear in mind that there can be nothing applied equal to it, as it is one of nature's own remedies...it purifies the blood, strengthens the nervous system; cures headaches, toothaches, neuralgia, and all diseases of the nervous system. Can be applied to a child six months old as well as to a full-grown person. Remember that electricity is life." [2]

Even the legitimate healers were subject to cause more harm than good to their patients. In October 1865, a Mexican woman named Teresa Forjas, who had been ill for some time under a doctor's care, sent her friend for some quinine. The clerk mistakenly gave her morphine. She died the next morning. The druggist was tried, but eventually released. [3]

WORKS CITED

1. The Roar and the Silence, p.198
2. The Big Bonanza, p.297
3. The History of Virginia City, NV Cemeteries, p.10

**Originally part of the Utah
Territory, the Comstock miners
were technically forbidden to drink.
The Mormon government wisely did
not enforce this rule, however.**

VIII

GROSH BROTHERS GOODS

**General Van Bokkelen, prominent
in Virginia City, stored miner's
highly explosive and unstable
nitroglycerin in his bedroom, which
was so packed he slept on cases of
black powder. On June 30, 1873, his
unruly pet monkey set off an
exposion that killed at least 10
people, including himself.**

Grosh Bros. Goods is a charming store on South C
Street that holds all manner of merchandise and gifts,
specializing in art and antiques. A small second-story loft
is accessible from the rear of the store, allowing
shoppers access to additional art and collectibles.

THE HAUNTINGS

I was visiting [Grosh Bros.] one early evening when it happened. My shop was next door, and I had already finished for the day. I walked over and chatted with my friend Tina as she was closing up. We were both near the main counter, myself in front of it, as we waited for the last customer to finish.

Our conversation drifted about as our eyes followed a middle-aged woman wearing a dark red sweatshirt. The ticking of the many high-quality antique clock reproductions sounded off our impatience for the woman. She stood before the massive armoire, a walnut masterpiece that rose massively all the way to the ceiling. Both of its doors had been removed and flanked the item to better display old clocks and ancient knick-knacks inside. She took her time reviewing some items on display there, and I found myself gazing absent-mindedly about the shop.

It was a comparatively small building, packed with items of all types and ages. Some steps in the back led to a landing, which turned for another few stairs leading to an open loft. The walls were covered with muttering clock reproductions and timepieces. This mixed with the joyful piano sounds of Squeak, Virginia City's local celebrity old-time pianist. Her style was unmistakable and of an era that had long ago passed into the sands and sage of the high desert. The many clicks from the clocks countered the rhythm of Squeak's piano as it emanated from the stereo speakers surrounding the shop. A large player piano sat forlornly in a corner, reminiscent of those bygone tunes… though the lid over the keys was locked down to protect the antique ivories.

Finally the customer departed. Tina switched off the stereo muzac as she passed by on her way to lock the front door. As Tina strode back to the counter, she slowed when something odd occurred. We both gazed upwards as the series of track lights that surrounded the shop began shaking. The light beams painted circles on the wall, highlighting artwork, and began spinning like searchlights. The entire series of racks rocked back and forth almost six inches, and we thought that we were encountering an earthquake. As the rattling continued unabated, however, we realized that nothing else was shaking... just the track lights. The whole shop was plunged into a surreal mode as the lights gyrated around and played havoc with dancing shadows. We frowned at each other, but were not particularly alarmed.

Suddenly Tina jumped in surprise. I gasped as an electric shock of adrenaline ripped through me.

Deafening loud, the sound of an old-time piano blasted through the stereo speakers where Squeak had just been playing not thirty seconds earlier. Tina put her hands to her ears and jumped over to the stereo behind the counter. I watched, also covering my smarting ears. Tina was about to turn off the stereo with a flick of a switch, but her hand stopped just shy of the receiver. Of course...the power was off... she had just turned it off a minute ago!

Her eyes met mine, wide with surprise. Both of us started looking around the shop, wondering somehow if the noise was our imagination, or if we could see some physical sign of strange behavior. The music was no longer specifically Squeak's piano... though still the sounds of an old-time piano... like the huge player piano sitting alone against the wall. There was no mistaking the late 1800's style. My heart throbbed painfully as fear wracked my body… but the strangeness did not cease.

Tina pulled the stereo out from the wall, and removed the electrical cord from the outlet. Still the music deafened us. The cacophony was all around us, through the stereo speakers that were placed in all the corners of the shop. Almost as if in a trance, I slowly approached the player piano. The lid was closed, so I couldn't see if the keys were moving. I wasn't sure if I had the courage to open it and check or not, but I found myself nearing it. Slowly I reached my hand out to pull up the lid, but I hesitated.

Did I really want to see this? The music was almost painfully loud… but what did I expect? The music was coming through the speakers… not from the old antique. Certainly the piano could not reach this volume on its own, and it was not connected to the speakers in any way. Shaking aside my fear, I snapped my hand forward to jerk open the lid.

Silence.

As soon as my fingers touched the player piano, the shop fell into a stunning silence. The change was so abrupt I almost lost my balance, as if I had been bracing against the noise. I realized that it had been my bunched nerves, of course, which suddenly released their tension when the awful sounds stopped. The lights were quiet, too. My heart continued to pound mercilessly in my chest, and I realized that my ragged breathing was coarse and loud. Stunned, I gazed back at Tina… but she had no explanation either.

***

"I had a blind cat a while back… a sweet little thing. Anyway, she would play with ghosts. Outside my apartment was a foyer. On Friday and Saturday nights, in the foyer, I would smell lavender perfume. It was strong, and I got the impression that it was from a couple of girls. I don't think they were ladies of the night or anything, but just young women. When the smell was there, the blind cat would follow it into the foyer. She would sit there, then she would start to wave back and forth… back and forth… then suddenly she would jump straight up, like three feet. She would do this for forty-five minutes at a time, and I would just watch. She was oblivious to me, and seemed to be totally absorbed with someone else. When the smell would go away… it didn't fade, it would just disappear… then the cat would leave.

"I eventually moved to another apartment, on the corner of Taylor and B Street. This one was in a basement, but it still had a foyer and, no kidding, the girls followed me. I could smell the lavender in the foyer, and the cat would always come out and jump around and play with them.

"I moved to a third place, and they followed me yet again. This time there was no foyer outside my apartment, but there was a landing on the stairs that was the nearest thing to one. Sure enough, the smells came back, and here came Iris, blind as can be, but having a great time out on the landing."

***

"I have this ring… this was made from my father's Golden Gloves Ring. I got it when I was sixteen years old. I never take it off. In fact… my sister came up to visit from California. We ran around and all that stuff. When I got home, I noticed my ring was gone. I was heartbroken. I said to [my landlady], 'Glenda, I lost my ring.' I called my sister and had her look in her car, the whole thing.

"Glenda says, 'I'll tell you something. We've been married for forty-five years. My husband bought me diamond earrings when we first got married. I lost one. You can't replace that… it's sentimental! Remember when I lost my earring?'

"I said, 'Yeah, I do.'

"Glenda continued, 'Two weeks later it was on my nightstand… with the back on! I can tell you that my husband hadn't found it! You know who did?'

"I shrugged.

"Glenda leaned in, 'The ghost of Pat Heart, the previous owner of… this building. He was renowned for finding anything that people needed or wanted, no matter how hard it was to find. You tell him you lost something – he could find it!'

"I appreciated her story, but didn't really believe in it… until about two weeks later. I was reaching for my scarf, when I noticed on a pillow… right in the center… was my ring!"

Virginia City at one time had 6 breweries and over 100 saloons.

THE HISTORY

THE IRONIC END OF THE GROSH BROS.

For nearly all of the early placer miners, a curious blue mud inhibited their work. It was constantly cursed, spit upon, and thrown away. Everyone hated the sticky 'blue-stuff'. However, the Grosh brothers, Ethan Allen and Hosea B., identified early on that this 'blue-stuff' was much, much more.

These two young, upstanding men had a cabin in present-day Silver City, near Devil's Gate. They came seeking gold like everyone else, and soon ran afoul of the blue-stuff that everyone so vehemently cursed. "Instead of throwing it away… they wanted to know what it was. They took it home, put it in a mortar, wet it and ground it to a fine powder. Then they baked it in an improvised oven. When they found a small dark colored button in the bottom of their crucible they could hardly trust their eyes.

"Thrilled, they filled a beaker with nitric acid and dropped the button into the liquid. Slowly but surely the button disappeared in the acid-solution." [1] It was silver! This muck that all the miners had been cursing boasted an assay of $3,000 a ton, compared to the (still impressive) $876 of gold per ton. [2]

The brothers kept the secret to themselves, and continued working to gather enough funds to retrieve the silver properly from the earth. Unlike placer mining for gold, extracting silver required an expensive process. They quietly maneuvered to gather funds for this operation; careful not to alert the placer miners to the true wealth they were throwing away.

"On the 19th [of August] while Hosea was out prospecting he struck the hollow of his foot a glancing blow with his pick. The injury did not seem to amount to anything. Hosea ignored it. He was strong. The wound would soon heal. He forgot that he was underfed and worried. Erysipelas set in. A red line raced menacingly up his leg. He was wracked with fever. Sometimes he mentioned a stiff neck. The muscles around his jaw were tight, he complained. But that didn't worry the brothers; there was no [known] connection between swallowing and a sore foot.

That night Hosea grew perceptibly worse. His fever mounted. He felt chilly – looked blue. Allen was alarmed over the change in his brother's expression! Hosea's eyebrows were raised in surprise! At the same time the lines about his mouth were drawn out into a grimace - a horrible sardonic grin. He was suffering agonizing pain, yet he grinned as if he were going to burst with laughter. Chills shook him from head to foot. Allen could force neither food nor drink between his teeth. They were locked. Allen sat courageously by – ministering – encouraging – praying – until September second. That day Hosea died." [1]

Financially broken by his brother's death, Allen felt the need to cross the Sierra Nevada and into California. He knew that the secret he held, and his brother died for, would not remain undiscovered for much longer. As soon as he was logistically able to make the arduous journey, he vowed to cross into California to make good their dreams of wealth. With a companion he set out, but was unfortunately not able to begin travel until late in the season.

They were soon caught in a blinding blizzard near Tahoe, and could not find the trail to Truckee. This was quickly followed by another snowstorm, and yet another. Their provisions did not last long, and they were forced to put down their donkey rather than watch her starve. In danger of this fate themselves, they drove onward into the unforgiving, white-sheathed mountains.

"They started down the mountainside – half sliding – half falling. Snow-shoes were useless. They took them off. Threw them away. It had grown bitterly cold – blowing hard from the west. They found the trail. They lost it again. Allen felt weak. His pack was too heavy. He took off his heavy outer-coat. Threw it away. His blankets were wet – useless. He threw them away." (1)

They fought onward for weeks, living off the meat from the donkey... then on nothing at all. They were benumbed, starving, freezing, delirious. Finally they stumbled onto some assistance... a mining camp. Both Allen and his friend, Bucke, had legs that were completely frozen. The miners all recognized that gangrene had set into both men's legs. They also knew there was no doctor within miles... and no anesthetic. With a saw and a hunting knife, the miners removed the frozen, deadened legs from the men. But it was too late.

Allen Grosh died soon after, and took the secret of silver wealth in Gold Canyon to the grave with him. It would be years before the silver was eventually capitalized upon.

WORKS CITED

1. The Saga of the Comstock Lode, pp.16, 19-21, 24-28
2. National Geographic: Queen of the Comstock Lode, p.91

An early Comstock sheriff filled juror boxes with only fat men, or ugly men, or whatever suited his sense of humor. One 'tall-only jury' held such men as H.M.Vesey (creator of the Gold Hill Hotel), and a Nevada governor.

IX

THE GOLD HILL CEMETERY

**The Storey County courthouse
boasts a very rare statue of Justice
who is *not* blindfolded.**

The Gold Hill Cemetery is a lonely swath of high desert that fenced off the living long, long ago. There are several sections in the cemetery, each more forsaken than the other, all overlooking the lonely, barren hills of Northern Nevada. Those hills once teamed with life and prosperity, but now house little more than memories and remnants. The closest neighbor to the cemetery is the huge Con-Imperial open pit... also a reminder of the prolific past. Both living and dead alike cannot avoid the constant reminders of the Comstock era. Indeed, there are more dead residents of the area to enjoy these relics of the past than there are alive.

THE HAUNTINGS

This site is unique among all those covered in this book. I have not heard any ghost stories in connection with the Gold Hill Cemetery. However, this does not lessen its popularity among tourists, historical import, nor how powerful a presence the location has. The cemeteries of the Comstock are in fact the second most visited sites. The experience of the author while conducting a hunt is hopefully more than enough to warrant the interest of those seeking a forlorn experience.

In 1880, 75,000 gallons of liquor (chiefly whiskey) were consumed in Virginia City and Gold Hill, not including the 225,000 gallons of beer also imbibed.

THE HISTORY

The cemeteries of the Victorian era were viewed as gardens. They were places for contemplation and for the enjoyment of gardens and nature. The landscape used to be filled with trees, flowering plants, roses, and dense fields of purple clover. Not even a shadow of these historic gardens remains today, only the dead carcasses of old trees and overgrown sagebrush. The early community wanted the cemetery to be a beautiful oasis in the desert landscape and a dignified place to bury their loved ones. These 19th century cemeteries were complete with watering systems. [1]

THE TWO FACES OF GOLD HILL

At its height, Gold Hill once boasted a population of 10,000, for the mighty Comstock Lode was actually first discovered on the flanks of Gold Canyon. In January 1859 a handful of placer miners discovered gold. By August 1860, Gold Hill boasted 179 structures and 638 residents. By the end of that year it grew to nearly 1,300 residents. The city was incorporated on December 17th, 1862. Not long after this a rivalry with its much larger neighbor, Virginia City, began for the county seat of Storey County.

By 1865 Gold Hill hosted three foundries, three fraternal organizations, two newspapers, two banks, and four stage offices among its many other signs of prosperity. Millions of dollars worth of ore was taken from the many mines of Gold Hill, such as the Belcher,

Confidence, Crown Point, Imperial, Kentuck, and the Yellow Jacket. [2] There were some fifty mines in all. [3] With such prosperity, however, eventually came despair. By the end of the 1870's, the Comstock was beginning to play out, and the entire area suffered greatly.

THE LAND RUNS RED WITH THE BLOOD OF SLAUGHTERED MEN

During the initial boomtown atmosphere, if someone died they were likely to not enjoy a proper burial. "No record of deaths was kept. The mass of the emigration were strangers to each other, and it concerned nobody in particular when a man 'pegged out', except to put him in a hole somewhere out of the way." [4]

To further illustrate the harsh social environment of the Rush to Washoe, Mark Twain wrote, "The first twenty-six graves in Virginia City Cemetery were occupied by murdered men." By 1863, perhaps to mirror the heightened violence of the Civil War in the East, one newspaper commented upon the situation. "The land runs fairly red with the blood of slaughtered men, and homicide has become so daily and hourly occurrence in our midst, that when a day passes that is unmarked by 'a man for breakfast,' it is the subject of remark." [5]

One reporter for the Gold Hill Evening News covered a murder, two fatal mining accidents, a runaway coach incident, and was so threatened by a belligerent miner that he nearly shot him with a hair-trigger "big, dragoon six shooter, carrying an ounce ball"… all on his first day! [6]

The History

Even the volunteer fire companies took their rivalries to a lethal conclusion, putting a man in the grave on August 28 1863, after together extinguishing a disastrous fire.[7]

There can be no doubt that the entire slope of the Sierra Nevada is littered with the long-since forgotten dead, from murdered men, to mining accident victims, to diseased children. And though the nearly 10,000 people of Gold Hill mostly moved on to other booming economies when the ore played out, no one will ever know just how many actually made it out of the Comstock alive. The current living population of Gold Hill is merely 194... how many more dead than living reside on these slopes?[8]

The first elevator west of the Mississippi River was in Virginia City.

WORKS CITED

1. Comstock Cemetery Foundation Pamphlet
2. Virginia City and the Silver Region of the Comstock Lode, p.119
3. Virginia City... in My Day, p.5
4. A Peep at Washoe and Washoe Revisited, p.79
5. The History of Virginia City, Nevada Cemeteries, p.15
6. An Editor on the Comstock, pp.3-7
7. The History of Nevada, 1881, p.599
8. State of Nevada Demographer, 2000 Census

THE HUNT

My vigil at the Gold Hill Cemetery was different than any other ghost hunt. The reason was simple: I had not heard of any ghostly activity in this location. However, anyone who has been to this lonely, wind-swept hilltop, nestled in the high mountains of the Virginia Range, will know that this is because there is *no one there* at night. Therefore my main goal was to establish my procedures and verify my methodology. I had some surprising results.

This night promised to be an interesting one, as a powerful winter storm was approaching. I love the weather just before a big storm, though this one was yet many miles... and many mountains... away. Regardless, I was bundled tightly against the blustery winds that foretold of a blizzard. My usual logic was that anything worth doing is worth overdoing, so opting for a night exposed on a windswept, lonely mountaintop during a blizzard seemed appropriate.

I shrugged off the imminence of the storm. I had spent days in preparation of this night, including coordinating with the Comstock Cemetery Foundation. It was all set. I wasn't about to let ten feet of snow stop me. Of course, this was exactly what happened to the Donner Party, just thirty miles from here. But, unlike them, I was armed with modern equipment like flashlights and a cell phone (though mountain-top reception was questionable... earlier I accidentally ordered a pizza while trying to call the police dispatch). I was prepared. I'm sure that I (a middle-class city boy) have more street smarts than them (dozens of continent-crossing pioneers). I therefore ignored historical precedent, and proceeded upwards to the Gold Hill Cemetery.

I stood outside the cemetery entrance and regarded the expanse before me. The moonlight was brilliant, though the moon was only three-quarters full. I could see the entire hillside spread out into the distance with ease. Surrounding the silent, waiting hilltop were mountains in every direction... some near, some far. Far to the southeast and far to the west I saw the humble glow of silvery moonlight on snow-shrouded peaks. The entire north view was blocked with a huge sage-covered mountain.

I grabbed my pack of belongings and reached for the gate to the cemetery. I was mentally prepared for anything... or so I thought. Not only was the storm approaching at 50 mph, so was something else: a monstrous tumbleweed. This Goliath of sharp twigs and angles hammered me from behind. It blasted into me with enough power to slam me to the dirt. I was *completely* bowled over. It rolled on by a moment later, the wind fortunately taking it off me with ease. It stopped next to the fence, apparently satisfied with itself.

I rose and dusted myself off. So much for my making a silent, serious, and respectful entrance. I rearranged my hood, which had become filled with dirt, shorn sticks, and sharp things of unknown composition. Squinting warily at the offending tumbleweed, I couldn't help but be amazed. It was literally the size of my Jeep, if not larger. Before this behemoth bramble, and particularly the impending blizzard, I felt small and humble. As I walked by it, I couldn't help but take my own jab back, just to restore some dignity.

"Ha! I can get into the cemetery... and you can't!

So, like, who's the coolest now, and stuff, eh?"

I unlatched the gate and entered the cemetery, ensuring that the tumbleweed was firmly caught up in the barbed wire fence. With dignity restored, I turned to face the night.

My initial reaction was of wonder... wonder at the amazing amount of light. I had no need of my flashlight, or even the extra batteries that I took pains to bring. The silvery light covered everything in a strange, glittering glow that seemed to flatten perspective. Soon a blasted-looking area with shattered remnants of graves and headstones surrounded me. Sage was rare in this location, but very short, stunted scrub was everywhere among the sharp splinters of ancient markers.

These feelings of being miniscule grew as I steadily strode up the ascending path of loose dirt. I was soon immersed in the ruins of yesteryear's dead. After getting hit from behind once already, I was very wary of being so exposed. I felt alone here, very out of place and completely surrounded by something unusual and significant. The ascent sharpened, and I came upon a boundary of barbed wire. Beyond was a small enclosure filled with the best kept of the headstones.

Numerous obelisks reared before me at various angles, all thrusting themselves into the crystalline, nocturnal sky. It appeared nothing less than an exposed rib cage, broken and half-buried in the earth. Beyond the hilltop bristling with obelisks was the mountain, sage-covered and drab. A full third of its immense bulk had been shorn decades ago into an open-pit mine. The sheer sides of this massive gouge were hundreds of feet high; smooth white stone was exposed like a horrid wound. I could feel the awesome presence of the gargantuan pit, even if I couldn't see into its depths.

The wind was a constant reminder of how exposed I was. It tugged at the barbed wire and whistled as it flew by, and the sage shivered from the chill. Yet another blast of wind hammered into me, and I staggered to the side, breaking the spell of the scene.

I decided to walk around a bit. I scrunched through the soft sand and dirt, and over the scratchy scrub. A flutter of the few sage plants rustling sounded above the strong wind. Then a new sound caught my ear... something very different.

I neared a cluster of graves smothered by a massive manzanita plant, nearly eight feet in diameter. Several headstones were bound in fencing constructed of fitted pipes. Nestled inside this huge plant was the source of the sound. It was not a sound that I would expect: it was not a rustling of leaves, nor was it a scratching of metal on metal. It was a tapping, a soft, gentle rapping, like that of a tentative knock upon a door.

I circled the enclosure, and leaned closer. A large, wide headstone peaked from the dark green embrace of the shrub. It had been broken from its base long ago. Nearby came the rapping. It was gentle and consistent. I concluded soon that it was just some hidden object being manipulated by the wind. I certainly wasn't going to dive into the shrub to discover what. And, more importantly, I didn't like how the manzanita reminded me of the tumbleweed at the gate.

I sighed, and looked to the sky above me. The stars were sharp pinpoints of light, but it was the moon that captivated me. Surrounding the waxing orb was a blue ring: the old telltale sign of an impending storm. This was the most intense blue ring I have ever seen surrounding the moon, however. It was so thick and tangible that it appeared solid. In fact, there were two of them: both hugging the moon close. It was surreally beautiful.

I meandered down the hill a bit, and continued my wanderings. I remained silent, and just tried to stay open to what was going on around me. I let my mind be free. It was easy to do: there was no escaping the emotions of this location. In every other cemetery I've been in, I might as well be in Wal-Mart for all the feelings I encounter. Not so with this forlorn place. I trailed my gloved fingers along a metal railing with peeling white paint as I started down a steep decline beside it.

Then I saw it. I missed a step. The loose dirt beneath me began sliding down the hill, and I struggled to maintain my footing. Sand poured into the tops of my boots as I planted them. Finally, after halting my descent, I struggled back up the steep earthen incline and stared in wonder.

From higher up the hill, near the cluster of graves that I had just been observing, was a shimmering white light. It was huge and bright: it was nothing less than a spotlight emanating from the center of the cemetery's dark, jutting obelisks. It almost hurt to stare at this blazing white brilliance, fringed with green.

This was it! Rumors of glowing headstones came to memory, though they were all from other cemeteries. I stared, stunned. Seconds passed, and the light did not fade. What was this? Was it a restless spirit, demanding attention from a world that no longer acknowledged it? Or was it a doorway of some sort? A portal? It looked just like a doorway into the afterlife itself.

Wait a minute. The doorway to the afterlife?

What was I supposed to do now? Go into the light? I

vaguely recalled that I was supposed to stay away from the light. Or was it the other way around? My heart began to pound faster as various theories sparred in my mind. Only for a moment did I ponder that it may, in fact, be some sort of explainable phenomenon. It could be an emanation from an alien spacecraft, for example, but I discounted this immediately. I knew the portal to Hades when I saw it.

I leaned forward, my gaze going deeper and deeper into the light. It remained there, waiting for me to enter into it. It beckoned me. But there was no way I was going to enter that light. What if I didn't return? I haven't even been to Graceland yet! I haven't been anywhere! Firmly I resolved to not enter the light. To prove my resolution to stay put, I sat down right where I was.

The light vanished. I blinked in surprise, but it did not return. What did I do?

Sitting there in the dirt, gazing up at the silhouettes of graves against the backdrop of the sky, I realized what I had seen. I contained my disappointment admirably. It was not the gateway into the afterlife, after all: it was the moon's reflection off the highly polished face of a headstone. To prove my theory, I stood up. Sure enough, the light blasted into my eyes. Graceland was in my future, after all.

I cranked my head all the way back to view the moon above. It was amazing how bright that reflection was. I gasped upon seeing Luna's curves. The ring of blue that foretold the oncoming blizzard was still there: thick and solid as can be. But to my utter surprise, it was no less than twenty times further out from the silver orb than just two minutes ago. Amazing!

I continued wandering and found myself in the

southeast corner of the cemetery. Here was a large grouping of fenced-in graves. As I neared them a line of mangled barbed wire suddenly materialized right in front of my chest. I stopped abruptly, mere inches from its rusty hooks. With only the night sky as a backdrop, I had not seen it. It was a solitary, orphaned line of wire, since the bottom lines had been trampled into the earth. I eased around it, and waded into a sea of splintered timber.

The wooden fence posts and vertical slats were all weathered and ancient. My gaze passed along the decrepit fences, one after another. A few had recognizable headstones within, but most were filled only with scrub and memories. This area, more than any other, reminded me that it was in the mid 19th century that these graves were placed here. The names and age of death listed on the markers was a cold enough reminder, but these unkempt, wooden remnants seemed so old, so forgotten.

Silently and resolutely I stood among these markers. I found it difficult to view the contents of the graveyard… my eyes wanted to scan the horizon to the far southeast, where the Pine Nut Mountains loomed with snow, so far away. This hilltop was for reflection, I felt, and not for mourning. I cannot explain these sensations. The wind, to my utter surprise, died to a thin whisper that fingered the wooden posts and murmured through the slats until it, too, felt the need to be silent and respectful.

Then I nearly had a heart attack.

A frantic, mad clacking burst through the serenity. I leapt back nearly a yard: the sound came from right at my feet! This horrendously loud banging reminded me of the noise a playing card makes when inserted into bicycle spokes. My heart was throbbing, and my breath was ragged from the cruel reflex that ripped through me.

I stood there, mesmerized, as the noise apparently tried to frighten me off. I frowned, and stared down at the gravesite before me. It was obviously the source of the sound, but I saw no movement whatsoever. Nothing. There was more than enough light to see all, but I leaned closer anyway. The hectic clapping continued, unfazed.

After several long moments of study, I identified that one of the wooden slats was, in fact, moving. The entire line of slats was ancient, and most of them were no longer fully connected at both ends. This offending slat was broken near the bottom, and wiggled back and forth like mad. Strangely, all the slats were loose... yet only the one moved. I watched it dance and spasm for a moment, then tilted my head back and laughed out loud at my own reaction. The laughter felt good, but I noticed that the night swallowed it up very quickly, and it did not seem to carry beyond the immediate radius of graves.

The wind began to blow again, and my laughter stopped up short. As soon as the wind started up, the wooden slat no longer tried to keep my attention. I stared at it, and thought hard about it. I actually stood there and replayed the entire event in my head. There was no question.

It had been shaking like mad during the complete lull in the wind... and had only stopped when the wind would have, in fact, logically propelled it. The storm gusted heartily, and I was pushed a step forward from its strength. The storm was coming, and I felt it wise to move on. I left the Gold Hill Cemetery in a sober, contemplative mood.

X

OLD WASHOE CLUB

"Everybody gambled. Even the
bankers and big mining men were
not excepted, their favorite retreat
being the sumptuous Washoe club,
renowned for its all-night poker
games." (Wells Drury).

This historic club was formed in the mid-1870's by
the elite gentlemen of the Comstock. It was an exclusive
social club, which allowed them recognition of their
status. It also was a way of avoiding the rowdier citizens.
It was formed in the heyday of the mining activity here,
termed the 'Silver Seventies', and rivaled exclusive men's
clubs in New York, Boston, and San Francisco. The
prominent members and guests included General
Sheridan, General and former President U.S. Grant,
inventor Thomas A. Edison, General Sherman, actors
Edwin Boothe and Laurence Barrett, author Mark Twain,
mining tycoons James G. Fair, John Mackay, and many
more.

THE HAUNTINGS

The evening was busy at the Old Washoe Club, and I was just one of many people in the establishment. It was a summer night, but cool enough up on the slopes of Mt. Davidson. The front door was open to the numerous people still striding along the wooden planks of C Street's sidewalks. The nightly wind that howled through the narrow streets of Virginia City, the famed Washoe Zephyr, had all but died. The howling of the wind was finished, but the baying at the moon by the people was just beginning.

I was playing pool with my friend, Pam. She was eyeing the table with intense scrutiny, and I absent-mindedly reached down to pet Phoebe, my German Shepherd who accompanies me everywhere. Her head was surprisingly not handy, and I quickly scanned the partially filled atmosphere of the Old Washoe Club for her. My eyes quickly found her some twenty feet away, gingerly sniffing at an empty bar table. An abandoned cigarette's smoke slowly wound its way up to the metal-hammered ceiling some twenty feet above.

"Your shot," Pam called to me. I needed little time to assess my next shot, as I had a very obvious and very easy move as the result of Pam's unsuccessful turn. I leaned over the table and my eyes followed my cue... but something made me pause. Something was not quite right.

I rose and scanned the Club again. Pam had made her way towards the bar in search of another beer, most likely. There were about twenty people in the Club, mostly along the bar with their backs to the pool table and me. A few of the tables sported patrons. It was loud in the bar, but a specific sound caught my attention.

Phoebe was whining with an amazingly high pitch… so high, in fact, that I suspect no one else heard it. She was near Pam, actually, but she was facing away from her. She was staring intently at the doorway opposite the room to her, some twenty feet away from me as well. I studied Phoebe in curiosity. She was sitting on her haunches, but she was obviously agitated. She shuffled forward awkwardly as if ready to act, ready to launch herself from her sitting position into some intense action. This was no game, I knew. She was deeply disturbed.

No one seemed to notice, but all the other sounds in the bar dropped away for me as I focused on that amazingly high, frightened whine. It almost hurt my ears. It certainly affected me… no one likes to see their beloved pet so uncomfortable. Reflexively I followed her gaze… and stared in absolute shock.

The figure of a woman was standing in the doorway. I say figure, as she was not completely present… her feet seemed to disappear just above the floor. This was not any ordinary woman. Her dress was period in design, and very worn. It is not uncommon to see period clothing in Virginia City, but her blue corduroy dress had the look of serious use and was not a costume. She was not wearing a hat… her long dark hair was loosely over her shoulders.

As I watched in mute amazement, she turned from me as if she had been about to step towards the pool table: she turned unexpectedly away instead, and stared straight at Phoebe. Her eyes bored into her from across the room, and a pang of fright burst through my chest. She leaned forward slowly, malevolently… and hissed. Her hiss was deep and guttural, not at all the sound I would have pictured emanating from this lady. Her face scrunched up in anger like a cat's...and she actually bared her teeth! How often do *people* bare their teeth in such a primal display of aggression? Then she swiftly floated backwards and *through* the closed door.

Phoebe instantly leapt forward and ran up to the door. She snuffled with excitement and pawed at the crack in the bottom of the door. She continued with these actions for I don't know how long, then suddenly gave up and trotted to my side as if nothing had occurred at all. I was stunned, and realized that no one else seemed to have observed this encounter. The bar was loud, and laughter rang out unexpectedly, making me jump. But that was apparently the end of the encounter.

***

Returning from the restroom, I gently closed the door behind me. I passed through the maze of tables towards the bar. As I passed beneath the angled ceiling, near where the steps accessible from C Street outside gave access upstairs, I felt a strong shove on my shoulders. I stumbled awkwardly, and loudly gripped a chair to avoid falling into a bar table. Frowning, I turned about to see who was so rude, but there was no one in the corner where I just passed. I shook my head and shrugged it off as a misstep, then returned to the only vacant seat at the bar.

I sat down beside a dozen others. Some were friends, others were acquaintances, and still others were neither. I took a sip of my draught and eyed the stained glass of the many bottles along the shelf. I absently gazed past the liquor bottles and into the mirror to scan the main chamber of the Old Washoe Club. My eyes found the former location of the billiard table, though now it was home to tables and chairs. Laughter filled the other patrons of the bar as I looked about contentedly. I eventually found the corner where I had tripped. I frowned. There was a figure in the mirror behind me.

A woman in an old-fashioned blue dress stood near the angled ceiling. She stood all alone, and seemed terribly out of place there. She was extremely petite, and her features very pale. Her eyes bored right into me through the mirror. There was an intensity there that was very unnerving. Frowning deeper, I spun about in my chair to view the woman directly... but there was no one there.

"What the..." I muttered rather loudly in confusion. My friend nearby pulled out of her conversation with her neighbor at the bar and regarded me. The laughter continued along the entire counter but for the two of us. A car's horn sounded on C Street, and a flash of headlights whizzed by in the darkness. It was winter, and primarily the locals were in attendance, so few vehicles passed by this time of night. The sound cut through the crisp air neatly, even through the old doors that led into the Club.

"What?" Michelle asked, apparently noting the puzzlement on my face. She set down her drink in concern.

"Oh, nothing. I just.... Well, I thought I was pushed a minute ago, but no one was there. And now I swear I just saw someone in that spot behind us in the mirror. Did you see a lady in a blue dress?"

Michelle chuckled and took up her beer once again. "Oh, you mean the Lady in Blue."

"That's what I said."

"No, that's what people call her. She's a ghost."

My shoulders dropped. Somehow I knew she wasn't kidding. "Excuse me?

"Yeah, she's a ghost. The Lady in Blue. Ask anybody."

"She was glaring at me. I think she pushed me as I walked by."

Michelle chuckled again. "Yeah, she's been known to do that. She is very particular about who she likes and dislikes. I have never seen her myself, but I know the story."

"Tell me."

"Well," Michelle began slowly. "There are a lot of stories about her origin. As many stories as people telling them, probably. You know how it is. But the story that I like is this one. Some say that back in the day she and her husband moved out West to capitalize on the riches like everybody else. The gold, not the silver, this was in the 60's, before everyone realized that the silver was even there.

"Anyway, while the husband worked all day, his wife Lena met a man who was basically a pimp. She caught his eye, or so they say. He murdered the husband, to force Lena into prostitution. There wasn't much else she could have done out here after selling everything they had just to get here.

"Lena marched into the club here, where the pimp was working one day. Somehow, I don't know how, she killed the pimp in revenge for the death of her husband. The pimp's wife was working here, too. When she heard the commotion she broke a wine bottle and ripped Lena's throat open on the spot with it."

I shivered at the thought. Michelle's narration was so curt and matter of fact, but the memory of Lena's eyes staring at me through the mirror chilled me to the bone. I sipped my beer, but the brew tasted bitter.

"The spot over there behind us, where the wall is angled, is where she is commonly seen. That spot is sometimes supposed to be unnaturally cold, as well as a spot in the room in back, past the spiral stairs. She has been sighted at the top of the stairs leading to the second floor, too. I know of a lady walking up the stairs and right at the top the Lady in Blue appeared right in front of her and shoved her back down. Nasty."

"You're telling me," I agreed sourly. I avoided looking into the mirror again that night.

***

I was actually a bit nervous to go to the bathroom there. I had heard of some strange encounters happening to people that I knew. I didn't know them well, mind you, but you know how stories go. I had just assumed they grew with each telling, but it was still kind of spooky. The door was known to lock itself when people were in the bathroom. It had happened to my friend twice, or so she claims. But my boyfriend was just outside in the bar. He was only a few feet away.

I closed the door behind me, stepped over a small footstool near the door, and started walking over to the toilet. It was not a regular bathroom by any account. Sure, it had a sink along one wall, and a toilet separated by a recess in the back wall, but everything was very old. The shape of the porcelain toilet did not have the look of a modern appliance, for example, and the whole recess was actually on a raised platform. I lifted the lid to the toilet, when suddenly the lights went out.

Panic flared through me. I *knew* something was going to happen! If this had happened in a normal bathroom, I would have just assumed someone had accidentally turned out the light from outside, or the power would return in a minute, or whatever. But this was not a normal bathroom.

A narrow strip of light snuck in from beneath the door, glinting dully along the floor for just an inch or two before total blackness defeated it. I forced myself to remain calm, and took a ragged, strained breath in a feeble attempt at soothing myself. My arms lead me through the darkness. I started towards the direction of the door, filled with adrenaline and alarm, and my heart nearly stopped when my feet plunged downward into thin air with my first step. Of course, the step up to the toilet! It can be very disorienting when you miss a step in the dark. I nearly cursed aloud… but then I heard something. It was probably the last thing I could have possibly wanted to hear: the sound of movement.

Something was moving in here with me.

Scraping across the floor in the blackness, I saw a flurry of activity scamper before the small strip of light under the door. Whatever else was in this bathroom was between me and the door!

Panic overwhelmed me. I screamed and slammed into the door. Frantically I fumbled for the knob, but it wouldn't turn. I pounded on the door, scared to death, and screamed again. I clawed at the barrier with my fingernails… anything to get out.

Within seconds my boyfriend was on the other side of the door, shouting my name and slamming into the door with his weight. I, too, kicked and screamed at the barrier. Pain flared through my leg, and I swallowed my next scream awkwardly as the hurt enveloped me. My shin throbbed horribly, and I heard my boyfriend's voice rise higher upon hearing my own miserably choked scream.

I slapped madly at the wall where the light switch was, but I couldn't find it in the dark. I forced through the hurt to recall where the light switch was. The lights in these old buildings are always in weird places. I found the doorknob again in the dark and frantically yanked on it. My boyfriend kept hammering from the outside.

Suddenly light pierced the darkness, and reality seemed to come crashing to normalcy. I continued to throttle the doorknob, and was rewarded this time. I yanked the door open and stumbled out of the bathroom, tripping over a fallen stool underfoot. It was the stool that had been dragged across the room in the darkness to block the door. When I kicked the door, my shin must have hit it.

Panting, I fell into my boyfriend. We left right away. Now I hear that they don't even use the same bathroom.

***

See Location C on the map.

"I used to live in the building... for a few years, even. I just love that old building... there's something very special about it. I would lay awake at night and listen to the ghosts of the past. I could hear billiard games going on, and could hear the dancers from the big ballroom on the second floor. You could hear ladies laughing... so much activity going on. It was world-famous for its all night poker games… and you could hear the gruff laughing of men at four in the morning."

***

See Location B on the map.

"You aren't scared yet, are you?"

My father had a very annoying sense of humor. Even more annoying was his friend, Pete, who was laughing so hard at his lame joke.

"No, Daddy, I am not scared yet. Ask me again later, though, OK?"

He smiled at me, good-naturedly, and then pulled his sleeping bag a bit higher over his shoulders. Pete was already nestled into his sleeping bag, with his back to us both. I, too, settled into my sleeping bag, uncomfortable on the hard wooden floor of the abandoned upper floors of the Old Washoe Club. As I struggled against the unyielding zipper, which somehow made its way under me, Daddy turned off his flashlight.

Fortunately, it was not too dark. We were in one of the rooms facing C Street, which were pretty small, really. The windows were really tall and slender. The glass was extremely unkempt, and the light from the gas lamps down below projected up onto the broken ceiling in dirty, swirling patterns. The light was faint and yellow-brown, but my eyes quickly grew accustomed to it. I lay on my back, and thought about where I was, and whom I was with.

Daddy had convinced his friend Pete that they should

spend a night in this old building, just to say they had done it. I was the teenager, but sometimes I think Daddy gives me a run for my money. My boyfriend thought Daddy was crazy, so I decided to go, too, just to show off a little. So here we were, on the 3rd floor. Daddy knew the owners, and got permission for us to spend the night in this creepy old building. I don't know what I was thinking.

The breathing of the others began to slow, and I could tell they were falling asleep. I lay awake and listened to the lullaby of old building creaks and groans. The ceiling above me captured my stare and selfishly would not let go. The cracks formed intricate patterns in the dirty half-light. I nervously fingered my own flashlight inside the sleeping bag.

OK, I was… apprehensive. I wasn't scared, though. I felt very small and insignificant in this huge building with such dramatic history. Many great men had spent time here over the last thirteen decades, and I forced my mind to think about them. The many small chambers, laid out intricately on the second and third floors, all had their own tales to tell. I recalled the huge room on the second floor that had originally been a ballroom, and I imagined all the grand dances held in there. These happier thoughts were designed to take my mind away from the very dark, very decrepit scenery currently around me.

I couldn't help but think of my first impression of this huge, scary old building, though. The entrance was from C Street, and was up a long, narrow flight of stairs. The stairs were really a double set, because the main floor has twenty-foot ceilings. I counted twenty-seven steps to the landing of the second story, and another twenty-three steps to the third floor. There was a beautiful wooden railing at the tops of these two stairwells. All this was only relevant because of the story that I had heard about these stairs.

The former owner, I had heard, had walked right up to the top of the stairs when a ghost, of a woman, appeared right in front of her and tried to push her down the stairs. I recall looking apprehensively down that long, narrow staircase. It was black as night below, as there was no power or anything in this old building's upper floors. The deep well was so black. And to think, we had to lock ourselves in, just to prevent anyone else from entering behind us. Imagine that, locking yourself *into* a haunted building. I can only imagine trying to find the lock in the blackness with a *ghost* right behind you!

A sound.

My eyes opened wide, and I turned my head over to the side. I strained to hear the sound again, to identify what it was. My heart thumped as my eyes scanned the walls, barely lit with smudgy luminance. Huge sections of wallpaper were peeling off in sheets, and I saw a curled end bobbing slightly over the broken remains of a chair in the corner. A flutter faintly crossed the room to my ear, and I let loose a sigh of recognition and relief.

I suddenly, annoyingly, jerked awake. A startling dream, perhaps? My legs twitched violently, and I could feel the energy of surprise in my previously relaxed muscles. I had fallen asleep… finally. I had probably dreamt of tripping or something equally stupid, and my reflexes reacted. Is that what woke me up? My mind was instantly sharp and aware… there was no grogginess at all. My eyes widened as I stared at the cracked ceiling.

There was something in this room, it occurred to me. I knew it.

I could feel the presence… it was bitter, bitter cold.

The chill crept through the air and crawled along the sleeping bag. I could feel it probing into the warm recesses of my tightly wrapped bundle. The iciness filled my veins, too. I started to tremble from fighting the adrenaline.

I swallowed hard. I knew just to my right was... something. I could feel it as clear as the silence was oppressive. It was just a few feet away from me... between Pete and me. My fingers gripped the flashlight so tightly my knuckles cracked. The sound snapped the silence like a gunshot, and I took that moment to jerk my head to the side.

There, in the center of the cleared, empty floor... was a tombstone. It sat there, heavy and ancient, rising up out of a pile of loose earth. I would have blinked in shock if I could have, but my eyes were glued to the frozen, dim outline of the headstone. The weak light silhouetted it, and I could see the black earthen pile extend right up to the edge of everyone's sleeping bags.

My breathing became ragged and uneven. Daddy was sleeping still, oblivious. Pete's face was out of sight, behind the tombstone. Fighting to keep control, I kicked at Daddy through my sleeping bag. He woke quickly, and rose up on a bent elbow to regard me...then *he* saw it. His eyes were wider than I thought possible, and he stared in mute horror at the center of the room. I almost started to whimper when I realized I was not imagining it. Only when he heard me, did Daddy look over at me.

He didn't say anything, but gave me a long, meaningful look. Then he kicked at Pete, and whispered his name to wake him up.

"Pete!"

The word did surprisingly little to alter the scene in

which we found ourselves. The dark presence in the center of our circle did not vanish once the silence was broken. I saw some movement past the tombstone, and realized now all three of us were aware of it. Feelings of discomfort began emanating from the grave marker, and I could feel the pulsing waves of discontent. I shivered, and tried to shrink into myself... anything to get away from this negativity that threatened to overwhelm me.

Suddenly Pete ripped himself free of his sleeping bag, and tossed it aside.

"Let's get the Hell out of here!" he cried.

That was all the impetus I needed. I screamed at the top of my lungs. I let all my fear out as I scrunched my face tightly and let loose. The next few moments were a blur as Daddy rose up and leapt over to me. Pete was already running out the door and into the black hallway. I saw his flashlight beam hopping through the dark in the distance.

Daddy grabbed my hand and yanked me up and out of my sleeping bag. I was then pulled through the black, cramped corridors of the Old Washoe Club, past rooms filled with the shadowy detritus of days gone by. I saw a glimpse of a rent mattress, rusty springs sticking sharply into the chilled air.

Then my fears came true: we were running into that inky blackness of the stair well. I almost fell down the long, narrow flight that led to the street. I could see the erratic beam of Pete's flashlight zigzag across the wall. He was pounding on the door in his fright, while at the same time feeling around for the deadbolt in the dark. He was obviously too scared to stop and use the flashlight in a systematic search. It only took another moment for him to find the lock and he hurled himself into the street.

The Hauntings

I was still hammering down the steep steps behind Daddy. The small square of light at the end bounced around madly as I struggled to keep up with him. Finally we, too, burst out into the chill night. It was several days later when we picked up our things from the Old Washoe Club... during the day.

**

See Location A on the map.

We needed another magazine rack for the new store, and Scott told me to go ahead and find one upstairs in the old building. It was hot out, and we were working hard at setting things up before summer hit. I wiped the sweat from my forehead and stomped out into the late spring afternoon. The sun was painfully brilliant after so long inside. I ran over to the entrance to the upper floors of the Old Washoe Club, and worked the key into the lock.

I jogged up the dark stairwell and turned right. Sunlight filtered into this area through a couple rooms and down a hallway, so I could see just fine. The first room beside the stairs, which had an opening to a room with a window, contained all sorts of junk from the previous owners of the building. Equipment, such as bar lights, magazine racks, and miscellaneous paper cups, all had worked their way into this, the closest room to the door. I tiptoed through the maze of unrelated junk, and had my choice of three separate magazine racks.

I identified the rack I wanted, and had to plant my feet awkwardly apart and reach over several boxes to get it. The slender metal arms of a circular belt rack gripped my prize, and I had to wrest the rack from this cold, ancient adversary. As soon as my fingers touched the magazine rack, I experienced something very odd.

The unmistakable sensation of someone right behind me flashed through my mind, and I felt a very cold blast of air down the back of my neck. I shivered, and looked behind me quickly. There was no one there, of course. My eyes scanned the dark entrances to the many other rooms deeper into the second floor. Unlike this poorly lit chamber, the halls all led into blackness. Indeed, in just about every direction there were dark, gaping passageways.

I shrugged off the sensation as my imagination, and returned to my task at hand. I gripped the brass belt rack and tugged it away from the magazine rack. I pulled on the magazine rack for leverage... and a cold breath of air slid down the back of my neck. I shivered again, this time with a violent knee-jerk reaction, and straightened up. But there was nothing behind me! If I didn't know any better, I would say someone had actually lifted the back of my collar to breath down the back of my neck like that!

Suddenly I felt very uncomfortable in this place. I took a deep breath and, steeling myself for the sensation again, I hurriedly grappled with the items to free them from their entanglement. I hauled both of them from the dark corner and let the belt rack drop awkwardly onto the boxes. I was so focused and fast about it that I didn't notice if the breath came again. I fairly ran down the stairs with my prize!

***

"I think the Lady in Blue followed me home one night. I could sense her presence all night. I don't know how to explain it, but I just knew she was with me. Well, her or some other ghost, I mean I don't know if it was *her*. Yes, I had been drinking a bit, just for the record. Not a lot, though! I can't handle more than a beer or two, anyway.

I think she followed me home, as I was saying. I felt her presence with me even after I left the bar. When I got home, the garage door opener didn't work, which was annoying but not a big deal. But as soon as I opened the door to the house, the carbon monoxide detector went off, as well as the fire alarm… at the same time as 'we' stepped in. Too many coincidences for me to pass it off as anything else."

***

One evening I was having a drink with my visiting mother at the Old Washoe Club. I just finished in the restroom, and spiral stairs are right before you there. This was back when the ladies' room was in a different location than the men's, and all the weird stories of the door locking and lights going out was specific to the ladies' room. I was more than surprised to encounter something right here, outside the men's room.

It was night outside, and the only light was from the

barroom to my right. To the left was a big room, dark and silent, and the little nook that held the spiral stairs was also shrouded in shadows. I could faintly see my reflection in the dark mirror opposite me, but mostly I felt the presence of the stairs rising up into the darkness above me. I also saw a vision of something not there.

At the foot of the spiral stairs, blurring the actual flight itself, was a large bathtub. I could not make out if it was an old wooden one, or a metal tub. It was old, I distinctly noted. From over each edge, spread like broken wings, stretched limp, pale arms. I stepped closer, filled with dread, and saw the blank, flat features of a dead girl. She was a teenager, most likely, and the tub was filled with bloody red water. Between her outstretched arms the red water sat still around her small breasts. Her chest was not moving at all. Her sunken eyes stared up at the ceiling blankly. She had bled to death, I sensed.

I shuddered, then hurried back into the barroom and the light and presence of the living. I, too, must have been pale, when I sat down at the bar next to Mom. She was gripping her drink and regarding it absently while waiting for me. She immediately gave me a funny look.

"Are you OK, Vic?"

"Yeah," I said sullenly. She was more than used to my visions of things like this, but I didn't want to tell her about it. I have found life is much easier when I don't tell everybody about everything I see. The owner, Sherry, walked over to me from behind the bar, and gave me an equally funny look. She was middle-aged with long, curly black hair. Her button-down shirt was stained from some spill while working the bar earlier in the evening.

They could tell I was deeply disturbed by something. The clarity of the vision was profound, and I had difficulty getting it out of my mind. I kept seeing the outstretched arms, hanging limply over the edges of the tub.

"Vic," Mom pressed, "What did you see?"

"Nothing."

"You saw something," Sherry prodded. "And I want to know. I need to know these things, it's my building after all."

Mom set down her drink. "Spill it." Her tone had changed to a bit of jest. It was just enough to lure the story out of me. I always respond to humor more than belligerence.

"Over where the spiral stairs are?" I began slowly, eyes on the drink before me. I hunched inward as I narrated.

They both silently nodded.

"I saw a bathtub with a dead girl in it."

Mom gave a sour grimace, but Sherry was intrigued.

"Really?" Sherry asked. "You know, there used to be a tub in that location."

I looked up at her with surprise.

"Yeah," she continued. "It was a barber shop in the old days. The stairs used to be closer to the front. I have never heard of any girl dying there, but who knows? A lot went on in this building that we will never know about."

I nodded, surprised. "I guess."

Suddenly I stiffened up, and let out a gasp against my will. Mom frowned and looked closer at me. "Vic?"

Sherry, standing opposite us behind the bar, frowned as well, but her eyes were on the space behind me. She squinted, and cocked her head a bit to the side. She reminded me of an animal listening to something. "Is she here?"

I nodded silently. I felt my face go numb and cold. I

could feel the presence right behind me of the dead girl. She wanted me to turn around and acknowledge her. I could sense it so very strongly. I closed me eyes.

"She wants me to turn around and look at her," I said to Mom and Sherry. "But I won't!"

Sherry's eyes followed something behind me, and I could sense that the dead girl was stepping closer to me. "She's coming closer," she narrated.

"I know." Suddenly the hair on my forearm stood straight up. I was wearing a short-sleeve shirt.

"Vic," Mom observed, "the hair on your arm is standing up!"

My arm twitched from the sensations. It was my left hand that gripped my beer, but I quickly let go of it as the chill seeped into my wrist.

"She's touching me *right now.*"

"Your arm?" Sherry asked. Now both could see how the hair was sticking straight up, as if static electricity were pulling at it. I could feel the cold clamminess of her touch. Unlike before, I couldn't see her, but I could sense exactly what she was doing. I knew she was standing right over my shoulder, skin pale and cold, naked and dripping with bloody bath water. Her wet hair was limp around her slender shoulders and the ends curled around her small breasts. Those eyes, I knew, were still sunken and ringed with purple.

"Yes," I called aloud, "I know you are here. I'm not going to look at you. All I want is to enjoy a beer with my mom."

Before all three of our amazed eyes, we saw my watch start to move. It was a simple watch, nothing extravagant, with a metal band that needed to be pulled in two separate directions to loosen it. The watch was pulled up and away from my skin, and the first step of the metal latch clicked open. Then, as if by itself, the latch was pulled in the opposite direction and the watch was loose. Suddenly it was flung to the side and behind us. We heard it strike the stage in the back corner.

I had not moved my arm an inch. All three of us saw it clearly, as did another man four barstools away. He looked on with as much shock as the rest of us.

"Thanks for proving that you are here. Now, go get my watch back!"

There was a moment of tense silence. We were all waiting for something. After another moment, I felt that the dead girl had stepped back.

"OK," I said with annoyance. I was not frightened any longer. Really, I had not been frightened at any time. Frightened was not the right word for what I felt. "I am going to get up now, and go to the bathroom. When I come back, I want my watch back!"

I rose stiffly, and headed over to the restroom. I had just come from there, but I felt the need to get out of there for a moment, and it was the first thing that came to my mind. Inside I stared at my reflection in the mirror for a few minutes, then calmly walked back out to the bar and took up my seat next to Mom. My watch was sitting there, right next to my beer.

"Who found my watch?" I asked her. Sherry, too, was still nearby. Both looked at me with surprise as I latched the watch back onto my wrist.

"Nobody," Mom replied. "No one has gotten up since you left."

THE HISTORY

The Old Washoe Club has been many things in its long life. Though most notably an establishment for the Comstock's rich and famous, it has also housed a variety of other business, such as Con Ahern's Capital Bar, a stock brokerage, a stationary store, a hardware store... even a museum of the macabre. Eventually the second floor ceased to be a ballroom, and became a rooming house. The third floor likewise became office space. The B Street entrance to the 3rd floor at one time also held an apartment.[1]

THE CRYPT

The back of the Old Washoe Club contains a very large, very awkwardly-shaped cooler. This is filled with all manner of chilled alcoholic beverages. It is not ideally suited to this end, nor does its appearance invite the obvious identification of this purpose. The strangely long, tall, and shadowed chamber seems more appropriate for something more ominous, something almost unbelievable. Indeed, it *has* held a more sinister purpose... it has held corpses.

The entrance is from a corner of the room, between two rusted iron doors that are permanently folded back. The wooden floorboards actually start about five inches above the base of these ancient doors, necessitating their permanent state. Upon entering the chamber it immediately darkens as the only light source is already behind you: a single, bare bulb protrudes from the doorway at about shoulder height. The light crawls along the uneven stone wall that rises immediately before the door up into the darkness no less than thirty feet above. In the 1860s, Chinese laborers constructed this oppressive stone puzzle. The stones are broken, mismatched and ugly, with cobwebs filling the dark, thick, empty seams between stones. It extends all the way up to the underside of B Street.

High, high above in the darkness in the farthest corner from the doorway is a network of wooden steps and walkways. Their shadowy presence is also ancient, and undoubtedly of questionable strength. The undersides of these paths are stained with age and decrepit. This was once a back entrance into the Old Washoe Club, but when a kitchenette was built, it blocked off all but the first few feet of stairs near B Street. A wooden ladder was then built into the back wall to access them from below, as they are some twenty feet above the floor. Even in broad daylight this rickety catwalk extends into utter blackness, for there are no windows in this huge chamber.

To the right (north) the chamber extends into darkness as well, perhaps another thirty feet away. The whole irregularly shaped chamber is cold and dark. Lined low along the walls are wooden palettes filled with cases of beer. These extend into the darkness. This is where they kept the bodies of the dead when winter's grip on the earth was too tight to bury them. Months would pass, and the numbers of dead would undoubtedly rise in such a harsh, unforgiving boomtown.

THE SPIRAL STAIRCASE

The spiral staircase was featured in Ripley's Believe-it-or-Not as being the longest of its kind without a supporting pole. It was custom-designed and built for the Millionaire's Club of the Washoe during the 1870's, the period known as the 'Silver Seventies'.

The stairs were originally located near the front entrance to the building, rising to the Millionaire's Club on the floors above. The windows near the steps allowed passersby to notice the wealthy citizens entering the prestigious establishment. Currently the stairs are off limits to patrons, and the top landing of the stairs has been blocked off for fire prevention.

THE HIDDEN STAIRS

See Location #2 on the map.

Not all who entered the Old Washoe Club were actually allowed inside the Millionaire's Club, which comprised the top two floors of the building. It was an exclusive club, and it held many secrets from the public eye. Therefore, despite the prestige of patronage, there were those who did not wish to be seen entering or leaving the building.

A stairwell is hidden between the back of the building, which abuts to the west with another building (which faces B Street). Inside this wide stairwell is a secret entrance that would allow entry to the second floor. These steps were tread by any number of secretive gentlemen who were interested in an all-night game of poker… or any number of secretive ladies for hire. It has been said the large building nearby was the home of a great many prostitutes.

Clearly visible from the main ballroom, this deep, dark well extends from the earthen foundation all the way to the top of the third floor, where it is capped with an angled series of glass panels. The facades of both buildings are brick, with fine windows set inside. Currently a door from the upper floor of the neighboring building opens into thin air, providing a thirty-foot drop for the unwary.

WORKS CITED

1. Buildings of Nevada, pp.92-93

During the Comstock days, Virginia City had a population of over 25,000.

THE HUNT

On February 13th, I stood before the great building, looking up at its broken façade. Fat, generous snowflakes spiraled about me and clung to the gas lamps rising before the sleeping giant. A huge crack down the center of the building fairly glowed in the dying day, prominent with clinging snow on its broken edges. I was reminded of the creepy Edgar Allen Poe classic, *The Fall of the House of Usher,* when the entire structure split asunder. The cold bit deeply this evening, and the sun had just settled behind the bulk of Mt. Davidson, indicating a deeper bite still to come.

Through the front windows, facing C Street, I could just barely see the antique wallpaper inside, practically rolling off the walls in sheets. It was yellowed and tarnished with old age. Those upper two floors were my destination this evening… in the one place that perhaps hosts more ghosts than any other.

Access to the upper floors was from C Street. Upon unlocking the door I was overwhelmed by a great staircase ascending into darkness. This was already a bad omen. Most stairs that end in darkness are going down… not up. One usually *descends* into black pits of darkness and horror. Here I was, ascending into one… proof the world that I knew and was comfortable with was already being overturned… while merely on the threshold!

Having to lock myself in with the key and a deadbolt did not help my already sprouting fears of isolation. The sliding of the deadbolt left me in utter blackness. My little flashlight was feeling rather pitiful at that moment. I tried holding it up and next to my head, like the police do, thinking it might give me an air of authority. I stumbled against something on the floor and poked my right eye with the thing. Well, if that was the worst that was going to happen to me that night, I would count myself lucky.

The upper stories of the Old Washoe Club have been off limits for years because the building is old and in need of much repair. Indeed, I had to sign a waiver denying the owners any responsibility in even bothering with me if I fell through the floor and died. Being neighborly folks, they did agree to come find me if I hadn't returned after several days.

Many people wished to see those long forbidden floors, and I had many offers for companionship. I had rejected them all, boldly proclaiming I was far more likely to encounter something alone than with a group. However, while staring up that decrepit stairwell, I suddenly felt a cheery group of ten or so would be quite nice.

I eased up the steps calmly. The path was uncomfortably narrow, unusually long, and very tall. The main floor of the Old Washoe Club boasted twenty-foot ceilings, so this was logical. I viewed the top of the stairs with trepidation. I could see at the landing another long flight continuing up to the third floor directly. There were a whole lot of stairs to fall down.

Why, you wonder, would I worry about falling down the stairs? This was not a pessimistic attitude by any means. One of the first tales I heard regarding this place was of a ghost appearing at the top of the stairs and shoving a woman back down. That lady had owned the building, and had plenty of reason to be here. But me? I just wanted to see a ghost. Would I even need to set foot upstairs before achieving my foolhardy objective? Fortunately, if I did tumble all the way down I would slam into the locked door. Then I wouldn't have to land, sprawled painfully, at someone's feet... so at least some dignity would be saved.

I found myself counting the steps out loud, though quietly. I didn't want to surprise any lingering spirits, after all, so I made my presence clearly known. On the count of twenty-seven I set foot on the second floor. My gloved hand gripped the ornate banister immediately... just in case. No irate presences, just silence... and bitter cold. Apparently I was welcome (see Location #1).

I looked about the place, noting my breath was clearly visible. Worried I would not encounter a ghost, but wanting my night to be exciting, I waited for a winter storm to break before coming. The huge building shuddered under the powerful gusts of icy winds. If I could remain dry, I would be just fine.

From this location, several directions held options. To my left stretched a long hallway, both dark and cramped, leading into the south wing. Periodic shafts of light would pierce this hall from doorways, somehow having navigated their way from a room with a view. I could see immediately this place was a warren of rooms, most in darkness, all with junk. Directly before me the steps continued upward, and slipping beside them was a hall leading into the blackest depths of the building.

I immediately gravitated towards the front of the building, intent on seeing the rooms visible from the street. I strode through a room partially lit with indirect twilight, and stepped over a huge array of miscellaneous business items. This room was the closest to the stairs and, ironically, already the specific location of the second ghost encounter I had heard about. It was filled with magazine racks, boxes of paper products, and bar paraphernalia. I strode through it quickly to another room, connected directly via an open doorway.

Huge windows gaped at me, rising from floor to ceiling. Their twelve-foot mouths revealed a blizzard outside. The snow whirled and swirled about, and the buildings directly across the street were snow-shrouded. Above and behind them was Six Mile Canyon, filled with thick, chilled mists and low clouds. Miles below, the hills were tickled with the delicate filaments of storm clouds meeting the earth. It was truly an awe-inspiring mix of the dramatic weather right here, coupled with views of surreal cloud formations in the valley.

I was spellbound, and pressed myself against the dirty glass. The thick, uneven panes were chill to the touch, shivering under the onslaught of the winds. I placed my hands on the low sill... then observed this was the home for several inches of pigeon droppings. My leather gloves came away with a chalky white reminder that these ruined halls were still occupied by the living after all. Well, if this was as bad as my night got, I was in luck.

I turned and began a perusal of the general layout of the building. The front façade had numerous rooms, all identical, and it was easy to see that the front half of this floor was bilaterally symmetrical. One room had amazing, aged golden wallpaper that looked like the surface of a pond with all its ripples shimmering in the dusk light. Nearby was a room with a window way up high that led into the back of the house. It was a huge horizontal portal, completely black on the other side since it led simply to another room. There were many of these strange windows, none of which served any obvious purpose.

Then I saw what was quite likely the scariest thing I

had ever witnessed in my short life. A closet was overflowing with raw electrical wires sprouting from some sort of patch panel. It resembled a tentacled, electrical Kraken. Mental images of Perseus combating the beast flashed across my mind.

Upon more reflection, I think this was the prop used in *The Empire Strikes Back* to torture Han Solo. I resolved that I was not the stuff of Greek myth, and certainly not on par with Harrison Ford... so I didn't step within five feet of that deadly thing.

I was forced to stretch a long step over some wooden planks to return to the main hallway. A long-dead pigeon immediately jumped directly beneath my descending foot. That was absurd... more likely its last effort in life was to land exactly where I would someday need to step.

Hopping awkwardly over this fallen specimen of clairvoyant ornithology, I entered a very large room at the end of the hall. This was obviously the grand ballroom at one time. It was huge, starting at C Street and extending over a hundred feet in total length. The ceilings were bereft of chandeliers, but I had heard they were now downstairs in the bar. Dark shapes were everywhere, most covered with sheets and all covered in dust. Stacks of chairs rose into the air, angling steeper the higher they stretched, and boxes enjoyed a population explosion.

Light from the outside gas lamps clung to the ceiling... along with the cobwebs... unusually white due to the snows. My flashlight was not needed here, which was fortunate: it was certainly not powerful enough to take in this whole, grand chamber.

I was startled to see in the rear of the room there was a series of finished windows that mirrored the C Street façade. These, however, revealed another building merely ten feet away, also with an attractive, windowed façade. I strode over and peered down into the depths between the buildings. It was a dark pit and my light revealed little… certainly not the bottom!

A long length of wooden stairs rose from the blackness to the right, and doubled back after a narrow landing on the far left. A series of doors from the other building occasionally met up with these steps… but not always. One door hung suspended in the freezing air… some twenty feet above where the light ended. High above was an angled series of glass panels. I could hear the heavy snow tapping against the ancient skylight (see Location #2).

This, I realized, was the secret staircase I had heard about. I could not see where they began on the main floor, but there was an obvious doorway from the dance hall here. I had heard the main floor access was through a brick wall [I discovered later this was true]. I nodded in satisfaction, and strode away. This was cool. I was beginning to slip into explorer mode.

I strode through an archway, following the weak light of my flashlight. To my right was a series of interconnected rooms extending towards the main hallway. The left held a large chamber, barely lit by the dying twilight. Windows filled the entire wall, like some warehouse, overlooking the courtyard behind the Club. The filthy floor reflected dully in the failing light. Right down the middle I strutted, towards the windows to take a closer look at the blizzard-blinded courtyard. I could see a fascinating network of wooden steps and rails peeking through breaks in the snow.

I nearly leapt out of my shoes as a commotion flapped belligerently at me. In my peripheral vision I noted a flash of dark gray hurtling past me. I frantically whirled my flashlight about to see the action, but this seemed to cause even more confusion from elsewhere. Suddenly I was being dive-bombed by no less than four pigeons, squabbling maniacally, and trying to frighten me off.

I stumbled backwards, completely freaked out. Instinctively I covered my face (and crotch) from the onslaught. I backed into a pile of something unknown in the darkness and fell backwards. I smashed into the floor and was immediately devoured by a cloud of dust. The pigeons all vanished into nooks near the ceiling... leaving me to gasp in silence.

I sat there, stunned. First I encountered pigeon crap, and now pigeons scared it out of me. I knew there was a joke in there somewhere, but at that moment I certainly didn't care. I was too rattled by the sheer ornithology of the moment. But, if this was as bad as my night got, I guess I was in luck.

I rose and dusted myself off. I meandered my way back to the main hall, and then to my point of origin. It was now almost entirely night. I noted things were a lot creepier when there had been natural light. Now, with everything in darkness there was a sense of familiar uniformity. Before I had felt comfortable in the sunlit rooms, and had looked down bizarre, cramped hallways that led into the bowels of the building... a black place I had to *enter*. It was the act of delving that was so bad.

Wandering deeper, I heard an unpleasant buzzing sound slowly growing. It was the sound of electricity... a lot of electricity. My flashlight was trained on the floor, so I wouldn't step onto anything, like an old mattress, or a pool of rat poison. However, I wanted to scan the walls as well. This meant a particularly slow process of step, scan... step, scan. I was carefully placing a step using this method when suddenly I stopped short.

Electrical wire extended across the room at my chest height. I blinked in shock. I had nearly stepped right into it! The buzzing in this chamber was intense, and I played my light beam across the walls. Dangling from the ceiling were numerous wires and cords: some horizontal and others vertical... it was a veritable 3D maze. Many had exposed copper or other conducting metals. Memories of that Cro-Magnon power box earlier flooded my mind. That danger had been easily circumvented... and had been blessedly quiet. This place was humming with high-voltage warning.

Water was also dripping somewhere in the nearby blackness. I looked down in further horror, but was soon relieved... I was not treading through standing water.

I eased through the chamber gingerly... not wanting to touch a single wire, but unsure if I had even seen them all in the dark. Despite my condensed breath, I was sweating profusely. Exposed metal glinted maliciously. I nearly dropped to my knees to cross the room... but I was soon through.

I continued to wander the remainder of the second floor, but encountered no other dangers. After a while, I decided to take my explorations to the top floor.

I stomped up the twenty-three steps to the third-floor landing, and once again gripped the banister tightly. The balustrade was simply gorgeous with ancient, varnished wood. Several spokes were missing.

The top floor was just as imposing as the story below. The design immediately reminded me of the second floor, though near the top of the steps was already a major difference. A beautifully curved, S-shaped wall of very high quality slithered away… obviously expensive. I was very impressed, and I muttered so aloud. There was no sense refraining from reminding any potential lost spirits that at least they were in a nicely constructed building. The more obsequious I was, perhaps the better my chances of a polite, rather than violent, encounter.

I stopped beside a claw-foot bathtub filled with old paint cans. Both the tub and I were presented with numerous options at this crossroads beside the S-curve. Unlike my porcelain companion, however, I did not plan on remaining stationary and undecided for decades. I chose east, towards C Street. I stepped over a paint can lid filled with a slimy green liquid, and down a very, very narrow hallway.

How any furniture was crammed through this place was beyond my imagination to explain. I exercised my creativity for a moment to allow myself an explanation. How did furniture ever get into these rooms…or, for that matter, out. It then occurred to me… there may not have been any furniture in here in the first place! That would explain why the tub was in the hallway… it was lonely and confused. I was so proud of my discovery of this obvious answer, I almost took a stab at explaining why millionaires would spend so much time and money here if there were no furniture. Fortunately for all concerned I was too taxed by the previous effort.

The classy, windowed rooms of the C Street façade welcomed me cheerily. These front rooms, also symmetrical, were relatively clean and lit. The gaslight from outside had finally settled into its preferred orange glow. The snow had ceased, and the wind had died, leaving the living ghost town in a serene state. The canyon below fairly glowed with all the fresh snow, punctuated by the black dots of pinion pines.

Illuminated in orange was an old newspaper on the floor. "Friday, September 21, 1984... San Fran Chronicle... Magnavox Compact Digital Disc Player for only $299, originally $349." I had been hoping for something a little older and more noteworthy, but I was nonetheless satisfied prices had continued to lower over the last fifteen years. I forgot the paper, however, when I heard a surprising sound.

A dog was whining... and was up here on the third floor.

I was sure of it. I released the paper and held my flashlight tightly. It was coming from the stairwell, but I could tell it was not from downstairs. I stalked along the cramped halls, my light held before me with as much menace as a 4-inch flashlight could muster. I soon found myself beside the bathtub again. The whining was coming from near it.

I looked around in wonder when I realized the sound was coming from directly above me. I craned my neck to see all the way to the ceiling so high above. Coming from up there was the whine. I couldn't believe it. This was not some wind whistling through a nook or cranny. It was not a sustained moan, but many short yelps. I knew the sound of a dog in pain when I heard it, and this was absolutely, undeniably it. My heart ached upon hearing such pitiful pleading.

Minutes passed, and the mournful sound continued. My mind blazed through explanations, and discarded them all. That was a dog. I reacted when I started to hear the scrambling of footsteps. I could discern the clatter of claws on wood, as if a dog had come to an abrupt halt and was skidding. It grew louder… as if coming closer. I took a step back… and tripped.

The paint can lid on the floor, I realized. Green liquid splashed up my pant leg and instantly soaked into my socks and oozed between my toes. Angrily I shook my foot into the air, trying vainly to kick the tenacious liquid off. To my surprise, the whining stopped as soon as I started kicking. What, did the phantom dog think I was kicking to drive it away?

A moment passed in absolute silence. I even turned off my flashlight. I stood there, in the dark hallway, just beside the banister. Gradually my eyes began to adjust, and everything took on a monochromatic grayness. Would it start again?

My right foot and shin began to ache from the cold. They also began to burn. What the Hell was on my leg? Pigeon poison? Rat poison? Ectoplasm? I squinted at my wet pant leg. If this were ectoplasm, then I was in serious luck! Why a specter would opt to leave it on the floor in an upturned paint can lid was beyond me… but then, what would I know of supernatural thinking? But I had seen several similar containers throughout the Club. No, try as I might, I just couldn't believe the undead would strategically place ectoplasm to get the most coverage of the building like that.

Did ectoplasm burn like that? I was slowly beginning to think I was not so lucky tonight. Ignoring the dissolving of my big toenail, I continued onward.

I turned and walked past the top of the stairs. There was no hallway, but just a closet. Frowning, I stuck my head in and peeked about. Strangely, it extended to the right: a two-foot wide passage extended deeper into the building. The sound of dripping water emanated from this path. Curiosity flooded me.

I ambled down the tight passage with my irritated toes. To my right was a normal wall… but to my left was a bright green wall lined with exterior siding. About ten feet up were shingles, which capped this small shed-like whatever-it-was. I angled my flashlight up. High above me… easily another ten feet above this little hut on my left, was an angled, glass ceiling.

The skylights were of aged glass, and I felt rather vulnerable beneath them. I gaped up as I progressed. The caulking around those old glass panes was something less than modern. I seriously doubted it was the modern silicon gel used nowadays, with the guarantee for eternity, or your money back. Despite my desire to visit with those that might actually have a chance at collecting such an offer, at the moment I just wanted another five minutes of customer satisfaction.

My progress abruptly stopped. My thighs pressed into a chain stretched across the path to my left, just beyond the little green shed. I gasped as I flashed my light onto it. This chain was playing at being a railing to protect me plummeting down a hole in the floor. Not just a hole, but actually a four by ten foot opening.

What was this? This was placed here by design. Somehow I doubted the patrons of the Silver Seventies were bungee jumping into this pit for thrills. I prided myself on not considering… not even for a second… that this was a communal pit latrine.

I peered into the black depths. The only thing I could see down below was a spider web of electrical wires. The floor was not visible, but my light would not extend beyond fifteen feet. So I was on a chained-off walkway, beneath an old skylight, next to a green shed. I could honestly say I had not envisioned this when I was planning this exploration (see Location #3).

Below me was, of course, the 3D tangle of deadly electrical wires, undoubtedly older than my ancestors. I recalled hearing the sound of dripping water when I was navigating that tortuous chamber. Up here I soon found the source of the drip: an old black pipe that came from the ceiling and disappeared into the wall. It must have been run-off from the snows, since there had been no running water in this building for years.

I followed the walk, circling the large opening in the floor. Beyond it was an old apartment, decorated in decrepit 1970s colors, with shag carpet and cheap paneling. All the cupboards were open and empty. The floor had obviously not been vacuumed in a decade, and large sections of a drop ceiling were missing, revealing a network of electrical wires above the living room.

I tried to tiptoe through the empty apartment, but I had to quickly reconsider. I don't think my toes retained their tips at this point. My foot was sending rather ominous signals that they had been burned off. My pant leg was transforming into a white tie-dyed look, reminiscent of acid-washed jeans of the 1980's. This situation was bad enough without reminders of 80's fashion.

I exited the apartment, and noted a door led to B Street. Beside it was another little door that intrigued me. It was only a foot and a half wide. Opening it revealed an odd closet a mere eighteen inches wide, yet about ten feet deep. I have no idea what could have been kept in there… or, for that matter, how anyone got all the way in the back. It was perfect for either bodies or umbrellas, I guess. I suspect it was only placed there to maximize available space (see Location #4).

Thusly did my explorations come to an end. I meandered downstairs to the main ballroom, and righted an overturned chair. I dusted off the surface and sat down. With a grunt, I snapped off my flashlight. I remained there in the dark for I don't know how long. I closed my eyes and tried to remain as open as possible. Open was, of course, a completely relative term. Basically I didn't fantasize about anything, and remained calm and attentive to any sounds. There were surprisingly few in such an old, large building. The unusual lack of wind outside, coupled with the dampening blanket of fresh snow, were all undoubtedly reason for the silence.

Silence.

Openness.

Just my liquefied toes and me.

Suddenly I opened my eyes. I could see the silhouettes of the stacks of chairs outlined against the windows to C Street. Behind me was a deep pit between the buildings. I had a sense… from where I don't know… that I was not going to encounter anything. It was not just a hunch. I knew. Somehow, I was absolutely certain I was not going to see any ghosts here.

My eyes scanned the ancient room, a place once filled with laughing ladies and gambling gentlemen…now filled with just dust. After so much time in the building, I suddenly felt completely familiar and comfortable. I wonder if I had just been given the seal of approval from the nonliving residents. If so, perhaps I was a lucky after all.

XI

A STREET RESIDENCE

This true location shall remain anonymous.

Kit Carson (whom Nevada's capitol is named for) was the only U.S. Army brigadier general who could not read, and could only write his own name.

THE HAUNTINGS

I lowered the box to the floor heavily, and then straightened up to stretch my aching back. Too much lifting today... and I still had a long way to go before I was done. How I hated moving! But then, who doesn't? I lumbered over to a large easy chair and flung myself into it. I sat there in a daze for a moment, feeling the sweat tickling the back of my neck. The room was awash in blazing streams of dust-filled sunlight. I winced at the extremes of light from the dark, box-filled corners to the blinding center of the room. My body began sinking deeply into the chair.

The large bay window revealed a spectacular view of Six Mile Canyon, blocked by a skyline of stacked boxes. The day was sunny and warm, but not hot... actually the perfect day for a move, I grudgingly admitted.

I realized that I needed a drink. I rose up slowly and took only one step before recalling that the box-filled couch blocked the doorway to the kitchen. I trudged to the side door and outside, intent on the sliding glass door to the kitchen. Halfway there I paused and groaned, remembering something unfinished out front. With a further sigh I gravitated towards the small lawn by the bay window. It, too, was filled with carts and boxes. I knew I couldn't relax until I finished this one more small task, so I squatted down next to a pile of tangled cords and began unraveling them.

Movement caught my eye, and I responded. A reflection in the window of a woman standing right over my shoulder sent a quick tingle of adrenalin through me. I barked in surprise, and turned to laughingly tell the newcomer how she had scared the breath out of me. But there was no one there.

Confused, I rose and looked back into the bay window. I saw then that the woman was actually inside the house, and it had not been a reflection after all. Annoyed that some stranger would just waltz into my house while I was working out front, I stomped around to the side door. She had the look of the welcoming wagon-type, actually. She was middle-aged and wore her red hair in a tight bun. Her dress was of an old style that I couldn't classify, but was not that of the usual period clothing worn around Virginia City. I'm sure she was just looking for me and I didn't hear her call out.

Stepping inside the living room from the side door, I stopped short. There wasn't anyone there. I blinked, taken aback. Now, I had only taken a few seconds to cross around the front of the house to the side... there was absolutely no way she could have escaped through this side door without me seeing her. This door was the only way out, since the doorway to the kitchen was blocked. It was not my imagination: I had seen her too clearly and in too much detail. She had been there... and vanished.

I gulped in a sudden uneasy realization: my new home was haunted.

***

After moving in to this house, I had chosen a small room off the main hallway for my workroom. It was roughly square with a door to the outside as well as the hall... and was mercifully close to the kitchen for a beer if I needed one! I set up a table and rearranged the shelves and countertop to accommodate my business. It had been a laundry room when I moved in, but I moved those facilities elsewhere. I liked having the circulation of an open door leading to the outside. The room was sheltered beneath an overhanging tree and was very pleasant during the summer days. It would have been a perfect workroom, in fact... had I been welcome there.

I noticed one morning that my scissors were not where I left them, but placed upon my worktable right in front and on top of my project. I stared down at them, shaking my head to myself. Yesterday they had been there, too, but I had assumed that I had forgotten them at the end of the previous day. Today, however, I knew for a fact that I had not placed them there. I had no roommates, but the back door was never locked. Would someone enter the house to do this? Obviously, strange as it seems. The scissors had not moved themselves, after all. But what did the message mean?

I began locking the door to the outside, but this strange phenomenon continued for a few more days, then stopped abruptly. I promptly forgot about the whole thing.

A few months later, I found myself not working in there hardly at all. I would get splitting headaches while working in that room. They were not the usual throbbing headaches like normal, but this sharp piercing pain behind my ear. There was no overt reason for headaches: my work did not entail the use of chemicals or anything that emitted fumes. I had the house checked for various gases, natural or otherwise, but it came up clean. There was no plausible explanation.

So I stopped working in that seemingly perfect workroom, and found myself using another location in the house. One day my friend Andy came by for a surprise visit. We cracked a couple of beers and sat on the patio.

"I have a friend from the Bay coming over this afternoon," he said after a while. "You should have dinner with us."

"Thanks, but I have some work to get done by Thursday."

"OK, but do try to free up some time. She's a trip: she's a professional psychic. Don't give me that look! She works for the San Francisco Police Department. No kidding, it's about as official as a psychic can get, but a hush-hush role. You know how they don't want the public to know about stuff like that."

I looked at him keenly. "Really?"

"Yeah. She's got some interesting stories."

"I'll bet. Hey, why don't you guys come over here when she arrives? I want her to look at the house."

Andy's eyes widened. "Oh, yeah! You've mentioned some weird stuff has happened. We'll come over tonight."

I was in the kitchen when the door was rapped from outside. I opened it to reveal Andy and a very small, plainly dressed woman. She was a lot younger than I had predicted... being only in her early thirties, I would guess. She had short brown hair and glasses with horned rims. She smiled affably, and stepped in. Andy and I had a beer, but she declined. I showed her to the old workroom, and she stepped inside and looked around. After a moment or two she motioned for us to return to the kitchen.

"That room used to be the living quarters of a miner," she declared. "At least, I assume he was a miner, based on his look."

"His look?"

"Well, my impression of him. I also got the impression that the room was once separate from this house, and that back door was the only entrance to it."

This was great. She was absolutely right: in the old days several of these rooms were individual cabins, but they were long ago consolidated. I told her so.

"Yes," she said, nodding at the corroboration. "He was a prick, and he doesn't like you. I detected that he has tried to keep you out of his home."

Andy and I both chuckled. "I've heard of disgruntled spirits," I said, "and those who try to right wrongs done to them in life and stuff... but he was just your average, everyday prick, huh?"

She smiled.

"I also sensed something else... something less amusing. I sense he wants to harm you, and envisions stabbing you in the back of the head with something sharp. Not a knife, though, but something else sharp. At least he wishes to. He really is an angry type."

I stopped smiling. Suddenly the scissors lying on top of my work made a whole lot of very, very uncomfortable sense.

***

I turned about and stared in surprise. The pantry door was closed.

I regarded it sternly from the kitchen counter. I had been going in and out of the pantry all morning... and had propped it open for that reason. Now, however, the door was closed and the stool that held it back had slid to the side. Or had it been kicked? After all, I had just turned my back on the door... and heard nothing at all. There was no way it could close that fast without slamming... yet there it was, closed. No wind, either. How had this happened?

And it was locked, I discovered.

Perturbed, I strode over to the shelves and glanced along the line of little ceramic jars and teapots. The fat little blue one held the spare keys for the house. I popped off the lid, cupped the cavity, and dumped the contents into my palm. All manner of junk rolled out: paperclips, tacks, change, a few old stamps... but no keys. The whole ring was gone, in fact. I shoved the contents back into the pot and tried the one next to it. Empty. As was the next and the next... all of them were void of keys. That was weird: I know that's where they should be.

I went over to the door and tried jiggling the handle again. You know how it is, when you keep doing the same thing over and over because you have no idea why it isn't working. My eyes went past my hand on the doorknob to the little ventilation window at the bottom. I saw feet. I almost did a double take. I could see the ankles and the tops of the feet of a couple of boots behind the little foot-square window. The details were hidden behind the thick metal mesh, and dramatically backlit from the pantry light inside. I had not left boots in there! And certainly not with the toes pressed against the door. Someone was in there!

"Whoever's in there, " I called aloud, "better open the door, or I'm calling the cops right now."

No response.

"What are you doing in there? Come out!"

Still no response. I think I saw one of the feet shift, though. I walked over to the cordless phone and took up the receiver. I held it down next to the little window.

"Look, I'm not kidding! I'm calling the cops!"

No response.

Angrily I strode over to the counter to grab the phone book. I figured that dialing 911 was overkill, especially in such a small town. I started thumbing through the directory for the sheriff. When I turned around, though, the pantry door was wide open and the light was off.

***

"In the middle of the night I woke up very disoriented. Someone had touched me. I looked up and saw the dark figure of a man standing right over me. Do you have any idea how freaky it is to wake up in your own bed with a stranger leaning over you, staring at your face? It was dark in the room, but I could tell he was a priest of some sort. His suit was dark, and his collar was different. I could not see his face in the dark, but I'm sure he had a thick, full beard.

"'Am I dead?' I asked. It seemed the thing to ask at the time.

"He slowly shook his head. 'No,' he said quietly.

"Suddenly reality came rushing over me, when I realized for sure that I was awake and not dreaming... but he was gone. Now, I am absolutely positive that he had been there. It being a dream was just not possible. There was a lot of detail, despite how dark the room was.

Suddenly I realized that he was a Jesuit. I have no idea how I knew. I just did. I mean, I'm not religious at all, and not even exactly sure what a Jesuit would actually wear or anything.

"So I told my friend about it the next day. He's always lived in Virginia City and was very interested in what I told him.

"'You know,' he said afterwards, 'a while back the Jesuits took over St. Mary's. They stayed up at the MacBride's house, as that was a monastery. They also stayed in your house.'

"'What? Really? When?'

"'Back in the Forties or Fifties. That's why you saw a Jesuit. I guess he never left the house... ever.'"

***

The wind hammered the house relentlessly, and the light from the candles reacted violently. The orange and yellow patterns on the walls hopped about, and the darker shadows from the smoky flames roiled in somber shades to blend into the blackness beyond the light. The candles were the only light in the living room, as the drapes were all pulled tightly shut to keep out the bitter night. It was snowing outside, and we wanted to remain as snug as possible.

There were five candles lighting the chamber... entirely insufficient to illuminate the entire living room, but each was designated for a person in the room. Tonight we were going to conduct a séance... my friends' idea entirely. I had already come to the conclusion that my house was haunted by not only one, but possibly several spirits. They all wanted to experiment with this rare opportunity to commune with the dead. Seeing that it was Halloween night, it seemed the appropriate time. I was not particularly amused with this whole idea, but I didn't want to be a spoilsport.

The Ouiji board sat in the center of the room on the floor, and two of my friends sat cross-legged about it. The bulky figures of John and Tim were starkly lit from leaning over the candles: their serious faces bright and their backs shady. Chris, Dave, and I were sitting on the chairs behind and around them, waiting.

"Maybe we should have the drapes open," Dave suggested. "It's kind of a blizzard outside, and that seems kind of appropriate."

Everybody shrugged, so I rose and pulled back the drapes. I tied them back and we all stared at the swirling snow barely revealed in the dark night. Finally John and Tim began moving the Ouiji piece about the board, and they began their attempts at communication. John's voice was calm and monotone as he asked some basic questions to the room in general. It was not long at all before the entire room seemed to respond.

The whole house began to shudder. It could not have been the wind: it was too powerful and constant. Plus we could not hear it getting stronger. No, the place shook on its own, and I immediately thought there was an earthquake. Picture frames hopped on the shelves, and the candles shook even more. The entire room took on a faster, adrenalin-filled feel as the fluttering light became more strobe-like. John and Tim continued their work, watching as the piece cut figure eights over the board.

Dave looked about excitedly, his eyes glinting even

more than his glasses. Chris, however, was not as interested. "Did you and Bob set this up somehow?" he asked flatly.

I looked back in surprise. "Yes," I replied sarcastically. "The earthquake was planned for 10:30, but I guess we're a little late."

The sustained shivering of the room slowed to silence. All we could hear was the gentle scraping of the Ouiji board's token sliding in a smooth rhythm. John gently spoke the next question. "Are you here, then? Show yourself."

Suddenly the drapes to the bay window slammed shut and swished madly back and forth. The rush of wind made the candles jump again, and our shadows contorted painfully on the wall. My eyes widened and the surprise caught in my throat. I had tied those drapes back! The gold braided ropes that I had used had both dropped to the floor... having somehow untied themselves. The waving drapes eased slightly as time ticked by much, much slower than my heartbeat. Finally they settled into a sluggish pattern, and we all started looking to each other for reactions.

Dave was staring open-mouthed. He loved this kind of stuff, and believed all of it. Chris was very skeptical, while John and Tim remained focused on the board. I was very uncomfortable. I knew the place was haunted already... I never wanted to do this thing anyway... and now they may have conjured up some sort of...

Suddenly there was a sharp snap, and the curtains silently dropped to the floor. The snow billowed against the window and streaked downward in the direction of the pile of drapes. The brass hooks glinted dully in the candlelight... bare and exposed above the window. I had really slaved to get those drapes on all the hooks…and now the drapes had unhooked themselves.

We were all staring at the motionless pile of drapes at the base of the bay window, when a sound from behind us made us all whirl in shock. The curtain that blocks off the kitchen was swishing back and forth… it, too, had undone itself. I saw the tie-down slither to the floor slowly, caught up in the swaying folds.

Chris was frowning, but I'm sure he could not think we had somehow staged all this. I gave him a shrug as I rose and walked over to the kitchen doorway. With annoyance at all this activity in my own house… where I would have to sleep tonight… I yanked them back open. As I reached down to retrieve the tie-down, I was attacked by a blast of frigid air. It howled through the room, and instantly blew out all the candles.

Instantly the blackness filled the chamber, and cries and shouts from my friends rose from the emptiness. There was much activity behind me, and I could very faintly see John and Tim rise to their feet, outlined by the deep blue, snow-filled window. Something made a ruckus near the wall, and I realized the side door had slammed open. Snow shot in and spit at us all, while the door settled against the wall.

I was near the light switch, so I snapped the lights on. The scene revealed was not as chaotic as the sounds had intimated. The confused looks on all my friends' faces were actually amusing. Their chests heaved from the rush of adrenaline that we all felt from the incident. I stared at the open door near me in shock. It had slammed open so hard that the doorstop had been hammered all the way into the wall. As I watched it dropped behind the sheetrock, leaving a dark hole. That door had been locked!

"What the Hell was that?" Chris demanded.

I shook my head. "I don't know! That door was locked… wait! The sliding glass door is open, too!"

I stomped through the house and noted that all the doors were open… every one… as were all the windows. Even the door in the old laundry room, which sticks and takes tremendous effort to pry open, was allowing snow to billow in unbidden. I flew through the house, slamming shut windows and doors…completely confused and angry. This may be fun and exciting for all of them… but this was my home! How much sleep was I really going to get tonight after all this?

When I returned to the living room, I looked at John. "Well, you wanted a sign," I said, "You got it! Now, everyone get out of my house!"

In April 1879, a local ordinance prohibited 'hogs and goats to run at large.'

RECOMMENDED READING

Bouton, Kenneth and E. Lyn. *Nevada Trivia*

Browne, J. Ross. *A Peep at Washoe and Washoe Revisited*. Paisano Press, 1959

Browne, J. Ross. *A Peep at Washoe: Sketches of Virginia City*

DeQuille, Dan. *The Big Bonanza*. Alfred A. Knopf, Inc., 1967

Drury, Wells. *An Editor on the Comstock*. University of Nevada Press, 1984

Diamanti, Joyce. *Queen of the Comstock Lode* (article). National Geographic Magazine

Ettinger, L.J. *The Best of Virginia City and the Comstock*. Self-published, 1995

Franke, Bernadette S. *The Silver Terrace Cemeteries* (brochure)
The Gold Hill Hotel Information Booklet

Hegne, Barbara. *The History of Virginia City, Nevada Cemeteries*. Self-published, 2001

James, Ronald M. *The Roar and the Silence*. University of Nevada Press, 1998

Lockley, Fred. *Vigilante Days of Virginia City*

Lyman, George D. *The Saga of the Comstock Lode*. Charles Scribner's Sons, 1946

McDonald, Douglas. *Virginia City and the Silver Region of the Comstock Lode*. Nevada Publications, 1982

Nicoletta, Julie. *Buildings of Nevada*. Oxford University Press, 2000

Nichols, Dorothy Young. *Virginia City... in My Day*. Self-published, 1973

Smith, Grant H. *The History of the Comstock Lode*. University of Nevada Press, 1998

Thompson & West. *History of Nevada, 1881*. Howell-North, 1881

Time-Life Books. *The Old West: The Trailblazers*, 1973

Time-Life Books. *The Old West: The Miners*, 1976

Time-Life Books. *The Old West: The Gamblers*, 1978

NORTHERN NEVADA

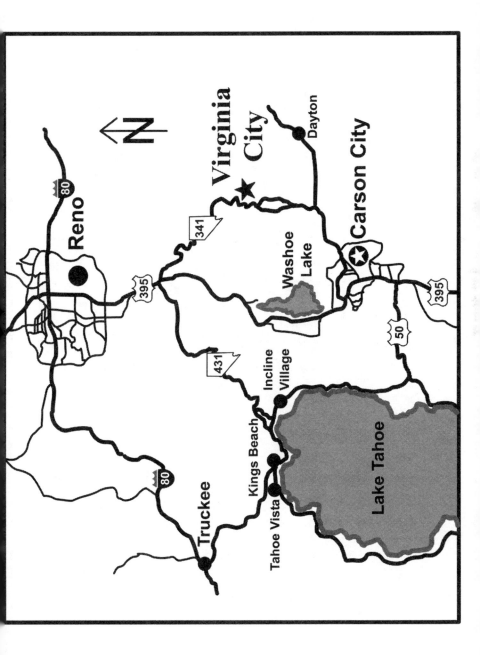

VIRGINIA CITY

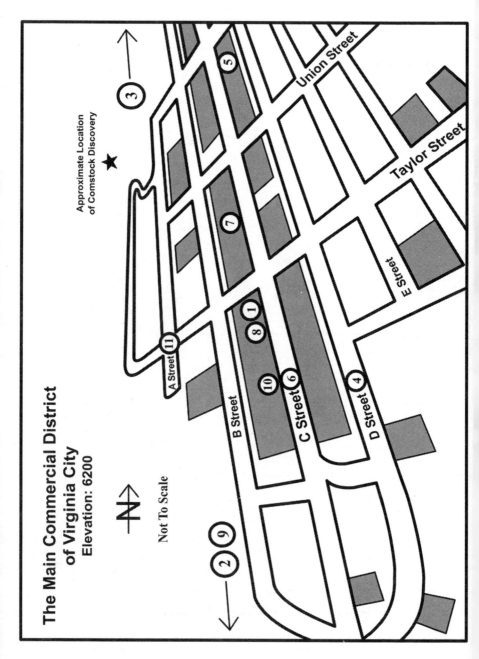

The Main Commercial District
of Virginia City
Elevation: 6200

N

Not To Scale

Approximate Location
of Comstock Discovery

Union Street

Taylor Street

A Street

B Street

C Street

D Street

E Street

DIAGRAM OF THE SILVER TERRACE CEMETERY

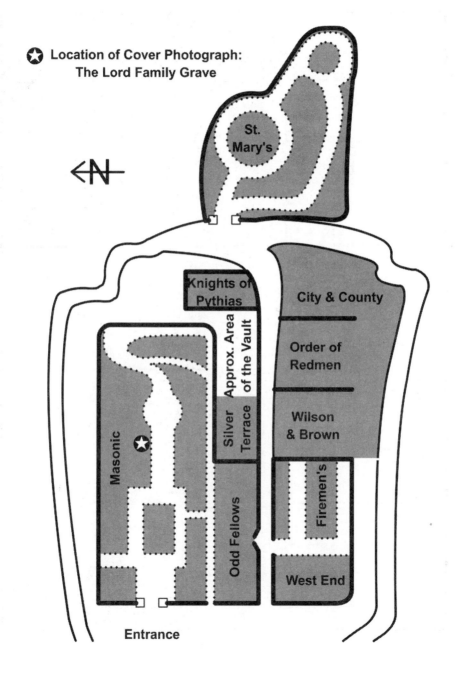

Location of Cover Photograph:
The Lord Family Grave

N

St. Mary's

Knights of Pythias

City & County

Approx. Area of the Vault

Order of Redmen

Silver Terrace

Wilson & Brown

Masonic

Firemen's

Odd Fellows

West End

Entrance

221

DIAGRAM OF THE OLD WASHOE CLUB

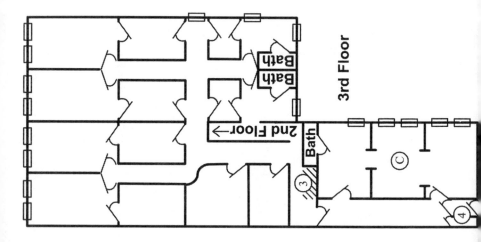

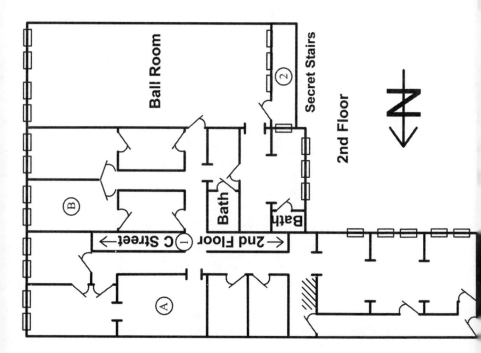